990
HAW

Hawaii and the
Islands of the
Pacific.

DATE			

04/20/04-12   5/00

**Cultural and
Geographical
Exploration**

Hawaii and the Islands
of the Pacific:
A Visit to the South Seas

CHRONICLES FROM *NATIONAL GEOGRAPHIC*

Cultural and Geographical Exploration

Cultural and Geographical Exploration

Hawaii and the Islands of the Pacific: A Visit to the South Seas

CHRONICLES FROM *NATIONAL GEOGRAPHIC*

Arthur M. Schlesinger, jr.
Senior Consulting Editor

Fred L. Israel
General Editor

CHELSEA HOUSE PUBLISHERS

Philadelphia

CHELSEA HOUSE PUBLISHERS

Editor in Chief Stephen Reginald
Managing Editor James D. Gallagher
Production Manager Pamela Loos
Art Director Sara Davis
Director of Photography Judy L. Hasday
Senior Production Editor LeeAnne Gelletly

The Chelsea House World Wide Web site address is
http://www.chelseahouse.com

First Printing

1 3 5 7 9 8 6 4 2

Library of Congress Cataloging-in-Publication Data

Hawaii and the Islands of the Pacific / text provided by National Geographic Society.
p.   cm. - (Cultural and geographical exploration)
Includes index.
Summary: Articles from issues of "National Geographic" magazine describe the history
and inhabitants of the Hawaiian Islands, New Guinea, Samoa, the Solomon Islands,
and other Pacific Island civilizations.
ISBN 0-7910-5443-8
1. Oceania Juvenile literature   2. Hawaii   Juvenile literature.
[1. Oceania. 2. Hawaii.]   I. National Geographic Society (U.S.)
II. Series.
DU17.H39   1999
990–dc21   99-28850
                                                    CIP

CONTENTS

"THE GREATEST EDUCATIONAL JOURNAL"

When the first *National Geographic* magazine appeared in October 1888, the United States totaled 38 states. Grover Cleveland was President. The nation's population hovered around 60 million. Great Britain's Queen Victoria also ruled as the Empress of India. William II became Kaiser of Germany that year. Czar Alexander III ruled Russia, and the Turkish Empire stretched from the Balkans to the tip of Arabia. To Westerners, the Far East was still a remote and mysterious land. Throughout the world, riding the back of an animal was the principal means of transportation. Unexplored and unmarked places dotted the global map.

On January 13, 1888, thirty-three men—scientists, cartographers, inventors, scholars, and explorers—met in Washington, D.C. They had accepted an invitation from Gardiner Greene Hubbard (1822–1897), the first president of the Bell Telephone Company and a leader in the education of the deaf, to form the National Geographic Society "to increase and diffuse geographic knowledge." One of the assembled group noted that they were the "first explorers of the Grand Canyon and the Yellowstone, those who had carried the American flag farthest north, who had measured the altitude of our famous mountains, traced the windings of our coasts and rivers, determined the distribution of flora and fauna, enlightened us in the customs of the aborigines, and marked out the path of storm and flood." Nine months later, the first issue of *National Geographic* magazine was sent out to 165 charter members. Today, more than a century later, membership has grown to an astounding 11 million in more than 170 nations. Several times that number regularly read the monthly issues of the *National Geographic* magazine.

The first years were difficult ones for the new magazine. The earliest volumes seem dreadfully scientific and quite dull. The articles in Volume I, No. 1 set the tone—W. M. Davis, "Geographic Methods in Geologic Investigation," followed by W. J. McGee, "The Classification of Geographic Forms by Genesis." Issues came out erratically—three in 1889, five in 1890, four in 1891; and two in 1895. In January 1896 "an illustrated monthly" was added to the title. The November issue that year contained a photograph of a half-naked Zulu bride and bridegroom in their wedding finery staring full face into the camera. But, a reader must have wondered what to make of the accompanying text: "These people . . . possess some excellent traits, but are horribly cruel when once they have smelled blood." In hopes of expanding circulation, the Board of Managers offered newsstand copies at $.25 each and began to accept advertising. But the magazine essentially remained unchanged. Circulation rose only slightly.

In January 1898, shortly after Gardiner Greene Hubbard's death, his son-in-law Alexander Graham Bell (1847–1922) agreed to succeed him as the second president of the National Geographic Society. Bell invented the telephone in 1876 and, while pursuing his lifelong goal of improving the lot of the deaf, had turned his amazingly versatile mind to contemplating such varied problems as human flight, air conditioning, and popularizing geography. The society then had about 1,100 members—the magazine was on the edge of bankruptcy. Bell did not want the job. He wrote in his diary, though, that he accepted leadership of the society "in order to save it." "Geography is a fascinating subject and it can be made interesting," he told the board of directors. Bell abandoned the unsuccessful attempt to increase circulation through newsstand sales. "Our journal," he wrote, "should go to members, people who believe in our work and want to help." He understood that the lure for prospective members should be an association with a society that made it possible for the average person to share with kings and scientists the excitement of sending an expedition to a strange land or an explorer to an inaccessible region. This idea, more than any other, has been responsible for the growth of the National Geographic Society and for the popularity of the magazine. "I can well remember," recalled Bell in 1912, "how the idea was laughed at that we should ever reach a membership of ten thousand." That year it had soared to 107,000!

Bell attributed this phenomenal growth, though, to one man who had transformed the *National Geographic* magazine into "the greatest educational journal in the world"—Gilbert H. Grosvenor (1875–1966). Bell had hired Grosvenor, then 24, in 1899 as the National Geographic Society's first full-time employee, "to put some life into the magazine." He personally escorted the new editor, who would become his son-in-law, to the society's headquarters—a small rented room shared with the American Forestry Association on the fifth floor of a building near the U.S. Treasury in downtown Washington. Grosvenor remembered the headquarters "littered with old magazines, newspapers, and a few record books and six enormous boxes crammed with *Geographics* returned by the newsstands." "No desk!" exclaimed Bell. "I'll send you mine." That afternoon, delivery men brought Grosvenor a large walnut rolltop and the new editor began to implement Bell's instructions—to transform the magazine from one of cold geographic fact "expressed in hieroglyphic terms which the layman could not understand into a vehicle for carrying the living, breathing, human-interest truth about this great world of ours to the people." And what did Bell consider appropriate "geographic subjects"? He replied: "The world and all that is in it is our theme."

Grosvenor shared Bell's vision of a great society and magazine that would disseminate geographic knowledge. "I thought of geography in terms of its Greek root: *geographia*—a description of the world," he later wrote. "It thus becomes the most catholic of subjects, universal in appeal, and embracing nations, people, plants, birds, fish. We would never lack interesting subjects." To attract readers, Grosvenor had to change the public attitude toward geography, which he knew was regarded as "one of the dullest of all subjects, something to inflict upon schoolboys and avoid in later life." He wondered why certain books that relied heavily on geographic description remained popular—Charles Darwin's *Voyage of the Beagle*, Richard Dana Jr.'s *Two Years Before the Mast*, and even Herodotus's *History*. Why did readers for generations—and with Herodotus's travels, for 20 centuries—return to these books? What did these volumes, which used so many geographic descriptions, have in common? What was the secret? According to Grosvenor, the answer was that "each was an accurate, eyewitness, firsthand account. Each contained simple straightforward writing—writing that sought to make pictures in the reader's mind."

Gilbert Grosvenor was editor of the *National Geographic* magazine for 55 years, from 1899 until 1954. Each of the 660 issues under his direction had been a highly readable geography textbook. He took Bell's vision and made it a reality. Acclaimed as "Mr. Geography," he discovered the earth anew for himself and for millions around the globe. He charted the dynamic course that the National Geographic Society and its magazine followed for more than half a century. In so doing, he forged an instrument for world education and understanding unique in this or any age. Under his direction, the *National Geographic* magazine grew in circulation from a few hundred copies—he recalled carrying them to the post office on his back—to more than five million at the time of his retirement as editor, enough for a stack 25 miles high.

This Chelsea House series celebrates Grosvenor's first 25 years as editor of the *National Geographic*. "The mind must see before it can believe," said Grosvenor. From the earliest days, he filled the magazine with photographs and established another Geographic principle—to portray people in their natural attire or lack of it. Within his own editorial committee, young Grosvenor encountered the prejudice that photographs had to be "scientific." Too often, this meant dullness. To Grosvenor, every picture and sentence had to be interesting to the layperson. "How could you educate and inform if you lost your audience by boring your readers?" Grosvenor would ask his staff. He persisted and succeeded in making the *National Geographic* magazine reflect this fascinating world.

To the young-in-heart of every age there is magic in the name *National Geographic*. The very words conjure up enchanting images of faraway places, explorers and scientists, sparkling seas and dazzling mountain peaks, strange plants, animals, people, and customs. The small society founded in 1888 "for the increase and diffusion of geographic knowledge" grew, under the guidance of one man, to become a great force for knowledge and understanding. This achievement lies in the genius of Gilbert H. Grosvenor, the architect and master builder of the National Geographic Society and its magazine.

Fred L. Israel
The City College of the City University of New York

THE HAWAIIAN ISLANDS

Fred L. Israel

Hawaii consists of a chain of 132 islands that extends for more than 1,500 miles. The eight main islands are at the southeastern end of the chain. Almost all of the Hawaiian people live on seven of these eight islands. The Hawaiian Islands overflow with natural beauty. Ringed by turquoise and purple waters, each island is surrounded by sand beaches that run from pure white to ebony. Inland, jagged volcanic cliffs are slashed by lush green valleys and deep gorges, snowfields, graceful palm trees, black lava, magnificent waterfalls, and the heavy scent of brilliantly colored tropical flowers. These attractions provide some of the most thrilling scenery in the United States.

There is another kind of beauty in Hawaii—the people. The islands have absorbed wave after wave of immigrants, each bringing bits and pieces from their homelands to create a unique people of a blended ancestry. In addition to those of Polynesian descent and whites and blacks from the mainland United States, Hawaii's population includes many of Chinese, Filipino, Japanese, Korean, and Southeast Asian ancestry. All of these peoples have contributed customs to what has become Hawaiian culture.

Hawaii has many colorful ways of life. Some of these customs come from the Polynesians who were the first to settle there. They arrived some 2,500 years ago. Other related peoples followed about 1200 A.D. Most of what we know about ancient Hawaii is contained in the oral tradition passed down from generation to generation. Both the physical and spiritual aspects of life—from the trivial to the momentous—became part of this unwritten record that chronicled both daily life and deep and moving human experiences. Another source for understanding early Hawaii are the journals kept by Spanish, Dutch, and Japanese explorers who stopped there as early as the 1500s. Together, there is enough information to affirm that the Hawaiians had developed a complex culture.

Captain James Cook of the British navy is credited with the European discovery of Hawaii in 1778. He named it the Sandwich Islands after the Earl of Sandwich, then the First Lord of the British admiralty. Other explorers followed. Cook had estimated that about 300,000 Hawaiians lived on the six principal islands but within 50 years, more than half died of diseases brought from other parts of the world. Gradually, western influences dramatically changed the islands.

Merchant vessels from New York and New England, then engaged in lucrative trade with China, called at the islands in the 1790s. As early as 1820, American missionaries arrived and, within 50 years, one in every four Hawaiians had been converted to Protestanism. By 1840, Hawaii became the main port for the South Pacific whaling fleet. Within 20 years, many American citizens owned permanent homes there. The economy was transformed. Sugar cane now replaced whaling as Hawaii's leading industry. Honolulu became a pleasant American imitation of a New England town. And, in 1851, the Hawaiian king placed the islands under United States protection.

The acquisition of Oregon and California in the 1840s boosted American interests in the Pacific region. Honolulu, 2,100 miles from San Francisco, became an important naval station, the halfway point between Asia and California. American residents had gained major influence if not control over the native government. In 1853 and again in 1866, American annexation had been proposed and favorably received by local leaders. However, in 1891, Queen Liliuokalani ascended the throne and inaugurated policies that strengthened native rule. Many Americans now urged immediate annexation by the United States.

On January 17, 1893, an American-supported coup overthrew the Hawaiian queen and established the Republic of Hawaii. Sanford B. Dole, the Hawaiian-born son of American missionaries, headed the new government. When President Grover Cleveland received word of the revolution and the use of some 300 marines, he, like the Hawaiian queen, reacted with indignation and incredulity. Cleveland sent a special commission to investigate the crisis. On December 18, 1893, the President informed Congress:

> By an act of war, committed with the participation of a diplomatic representation of the United States, and without the authority of Congress, the government of a feeble but friendly and confiding people has been overthrown. A substantial wrong has been done, which . . . we should endeavor to repair.

Throughout the remainder of his term, Cleveland sought the reinstatement of the queen but Dole and his associates refused to surrender power.

Queen Liliuokalani went to Washington to plead her cause. But, the United States was now pursuing an imperialist policy of "manifest destiny." The Spanish-American War was looming and Hawaii would become an important mid-Pacific base of operations to do battle with Spain in the Philippines. The timing of a "Hawaii for Hawaiians" argument was bad. Congressional expansionists cared little about such native slogans.

On July 7, 1898, President William McKinley formally authorized American annexation of the Republic of Hawaii. McKinley appointed Dole the first governor. Hawaii then had a population of about 154,000. No longer a curious Polynesian kingdom in the middle of the Pacific Ocean, Hawaii was now a possession of the powerful United States. Former President Cleveland wrote that he was "ashamed of the whole affair" and ex-Queen Liliuokalani compared the plight of her subjects to that of America's original Indian inhabitants.

As territorial citizens, the people could not vote in presidential elections. They elected one delegate to Congress who could introduce bills and debate but not vote. Voters elected a Hawaiian senate and a house of representatives but Congress could veto any bill passed by the legislature. (Residents would not have full voting rights until 1959, when Hawaii became the 50th U.S. state.)

Shortly before World War I (1914-1918), the U.S. Navy started to construct the great naval base at Pearl Harbor. The U.S. Army also established military bases on Oahu. After the war ended, the movement for Hawaiian statehood grew rapidly.

The first *National Geographic* article in this compilation was written by George C. Perkins, a shipowner, banker, governor of California, and a former U.S. senator from 1893 to 1915. His knowledge of maritime issues made him a prominent congressional leader in naval matters. For four years (1909–13), he was chairman of the Senate Committee on Naval Affairs. This article, which was written for *National Geographic* at the request of Gilbert Grosvenor, must rank along with those of Admiral Alfred Mahan in having had an enormous impact on U.S. political thought in the twentieth century. Like Mahan, Perkins argued in favor of a strong merchant marine, naval bases, and colonial possessions throughout the Pacific region.

One of the National Geographic Society's greatest contributions to the spread of geographic knowledge is its production of large maps, which are issued as frequent supplements to the magazine. Grosvenor borrowed the maps from the government for the first supplement, which appeared in 1899. At that time, the National Geographic Society numbered just 1,417 subscribers; as the society's membership grew, Grosvenor organized a talented research and cartographic, or map-making, staff. This staff designed and produced distinctive maps for the magazine, sometimes creating a map to commemorate a special event.

National Geographic issued such a map in honor of J.P. Thomson's article "The Islands of the Pacific." Thomson, a noted geographer, was honorary secretary of the Royal Geographical Society of Australia. His piece; Rosamond Rhone's pictoral essay on Nauru, now an island republic in the Pacific; and Junius B. Wood's study of Yap Island and the Caroline Islands were used by the Office of Strategic Services (OSS) during World War II.

We have also included Beatrice Grimshaw's article on the Fiji and the New Hebrides. Miss Grimshaw, an enterprising young Englishwoman, spent several years traveling here searching for financial opportunities for risk capital. In the course of her work, she explored unknown sections of these islands. Her essay and photographs are seminal in understanding the peoples of an area that would later be devastated by World War II.

THE KEY TO THE PACIFIC

By Hon. George C. Perkins
United States Senator from California

THE importance of the Hawaiian Islands to the Pacific Coast states is supreme. Those states in the future will rely more and more for their prosperity upon the trade with the Orient across the Pacific, and with the East and Europe through the Panama Canal. That there may be a guarantee that this commerce shall endure and increase in volume, the United States must be at least the equal in naval power of any nation using those waters for the transportation of goods; and a part of the power of a navy is supplied by its bases, from which all exposed points can be best watched and whence aid can be most quickly sent.

As such a base the Hawaiian Islands present advantages to us which have no counterparts elsewhere in the Pacific. Lying within easy steaming distance of our Pacific coast, as naval vessels are today constructed, they afford a point from which the whole North Pacific Ocean can be patrolled by cruisers, and from which the commerce Panama Canal can be protected. They afford a strategic point whose vast significance can be realized best by supposing the island in the hands of a hostile power engaged in war with us. From that point the enemy could send out cruisers to sweep from the sea the commerce of the Pacific ports and of the canal, while it would afford a base of operations for attacks on our Pacific Coast ports, as well as on the Canal Zone.

With these islands in the hands of an enemy, it is doubtful whether we could control the canal for a day, while the entire coast line of the Pacific states and the bays and harbors of our rapidly growing Alaska would be in constant expectation of a hostile descent. For the defense of our Pacific coast and its commerce, therefore, the Hawaiian Islands are vital, and this fact is recognized, I think, by every one who has given the matter careful attention.

In addition to the strategic relation to the Pacific coast of the United States, which Hawaii possesses, it has a similar relation to our island possessions further west—Guam and the Philippines. Hawaii and Guam are the ocean stations of the American cable between the United States and our possessions on the coast

THE CROSSROADS OF THE PACIFIC

of Asia, and as such are of vast importance in any scheme of defense of the Philippines or of the Pacific states. This line is of the greatest use to our commerce, and its safety can be assured only through means of defending its island stations against hostile attack.

And that commerce, which will continue to grow as the years pass, is not alone with progressive Japan and teeming China, but with our own fertile islands on the Asiatic coast and with the great English-speaking colonies of Great Britain in New Zealand and Australia. In 1893 our greatest authority on the sea power and naval strategy, Captain A. T. Mahan, wrote with reference to the proposed annexation of Hawaii:

"To any one viewing a map that shows the full extent of the Pacific . . . two circumstances will be strikingly and immediately apparent. He will see at a glance that the Sandwich Islands stand by themselves in a state of comparative isolation, amid a vast expanse of sea; and, again, that they form the center of a large circle whose radius is approximately the distance from Honolulu to San Francisco . . . this is substantially the same distance as from Honolulu to the Gilbert, Marshall, Samoan, and Society Islands, all under European control except Samoa, in which we have a part influence.

"To have a central position such as this, and to be alone, having no rival . . . are conditions that at once fix the attention of the strategist . . . But to this striking combination is to be added the remarkable relations borne . . . to the great commercial routes traversing this vast expanse.

"Too much stress cannot be laid upon the immense disadvantages to us of any maritime enemy having a coaling station well within 2,500 miles, as this is, of every point of our coast line from Puget Sound to Mexico. Were there many others available we might find it difficult to exclude them all. There is, however, but the one. Shut out from the Sandwich Islands as a coal base, an enemy is thrown back for supplies of fuel to distances of 3,500 or 4,000 miles—or between 7,000 and 8,000 going and coming—an impediment to sustained maritime operations well nigh prohibitive . . . It is rarely that so important a factor in the attack or defense of a coast line—of a sea frontier—is concentrated in a single position, and the circumstance renders doubly imperative upon us to secure it if we righteously can."

Hawaii is on the track of probably all the trade which the Pacific Coast states have with the rest of the world, and therefore, as a strate-gic point, it is of supreme importance that it be joined to us "by hooks of steel" which it would take the navies of the world to break.

The relation of a strategic point like Hawaii to the safety of the nation is illustrated by the relation of Gibraltar and Malta to the safety of Great Britain. The control of the Mediterranean is essential to England, as thereby she dominates the coasts of all the adjacent countries and controls hostile movements. "If," writes Lord Brassey, "we are resolved to retain our hold on the Mediterranean, it is imperatively necessary that our two naval bases at Malta and Gibraltar should be made secure from attack and efficient for the repair and protection of the fleet. In Malta and Gibraltar we hold strategical positions of the utmost importance." They are of utmost importance because they control the trade route through the Suez Canal, dominate the coasts of what may at some time be hostile nations, and render unnecessary the constant presence in the Mediterranean of a fleet of overwhelming strength. That strength may be safely confided to the channel and home fleets, which, with bases in that sea, can at any time secure control of it.

"If we abandon the Mediterranean," says Lord Brassey, "we cease to be a first-class power in Europe. . . . Upon a consideration of all the circumstances, it is clear that the dignity, the wealth, and the influence of England for peace depend on the retention of a paramount position as a naval power in the Mediterranean. We have that position now, and the recent manifestations of popular sentiment have shown that we are resolved to keep it." In that last sentence substitute for the words "England" and "Mediterranean" the words "United States" and "Pacific" and see if it will not apply with peculiar aptness to our own position on the greatest of the world's oceans. I think it expresses the present situation with exactness, and is an unanswerable argument in behalf of securing to the United States the Hawaiian Islands as Great Britain has secured to herself Gibraltar and Malta.

These islands would not long remain ours, in case of war with a sea power, if they remain in the condition in which they now are. Gibraltar and Malta are the strongest fortresses in Europe. So should Hawaii be the strongest fortress in the Pacific. The President recognizes this, and in his latest annual address recommends an appropriation for the fortification of Pearl Harbor. The War Department also recognizes it, and recommends the appropriation of $1,100,000 with which to continue the necessary work. That this work should go on without intermission until we have established there an impregnable naval base goes without saying. The only thing needed is money, and I am sure that Congress sees the necessity of voting liberal appropriations.

Pearl Harbor is susceptible of being made another Gibraltar, where the largest fleet may safely lie and where repairs may be made at leisure. It consists of an elliptical lagoon 8 miles long by 4 wide, with a depth of water ranging from 30 to 130 feet. It is completely land-locked, preventing surprise attack from submarines or torpedo boats, as well as from hostile fleets. In the rear are mountain ranges 3,000 or 4,000 feet high, on the slopes of which are the military reservation, about 10 miles from the harbor, where a salubrious climate is secured. Reservations for fortifications, wharves, and all that is

necessary for a first-class naval station have been secured, and this channel has been dredged to 30 feet, and may easily be deepened much more and straightened to insure easier navigation for battleships, which work can be done, it is thought, at an expense not exceeding $750,000, the value of the customs receipts of Honolulu for six months.

General Schofield, in 1872, reported on Pearl Harbor that "it could be completely defended by inexpensive batteries on either or both shores, firing across a narrow channel of entrance. Its waters are deep enough for the largest vessel of war, and its lochs, particularly around Rabbit Island, are spacious enough for a large number of vessels to ride at anchor in perfect security against all storms. Its shores are suitable for building proper establishments for sheltering the necessary supplies for a naval establishment, such as magazines of ammunition, provisions, coal, spars, rigging, etc., while the Island of Oahu, upon which it is situated, could furnish fresh provisions, meats, fruits, and vegetables in large quantities."

Too much stress cannot be given to the fact that if Pearl Harbor is to be fortified successfully the work must be done in time of peace. When war comes it would be too late, and woe to us if we are not prepared for defense as well as for attack. It behooves Congress, therefore, to give special attention now to the necessities of Pearl Harbor, and to liberally provide the means by which it may stand forever the strongest bulwark which we possess in the western ocean.

THE ISLANDS OF THE PACIFIC

By J. P. Thomson, C. B. E., LL. D.

Honorary Secretary and Treasurer, Royal Geographical Society of Australasia

WHAT memories of the past the place-names of the coral-girt islands of the South Pacific Ocean revive! They bring to the reflective mind the romantic side of life; they recall the daring exploits of adventuresome enterprise on the part of those early navigators whose romantic career has fired many a youthful breast with hopeful enthusiasm; they remind us of the illuminating pen sketches by Robert Louis Stevenson; they bring to our thoughts stories of thrilling achievements in the piratical operations of that onetime buccaneer, Captain Bully Hayes.

They bring us face to face with primitive life in all its varied phases, ranging from the nomadic peregrinations of the native trader to the precarious existence of the beach-comber; from the reef harvesters to the tribal councilors, and from the wild head-hunters to the bush cannibals; from the excited warriors, in all their fantastic accouterments, to the primitive village maiden, bedecked in garlands of wild flowers and habited in the simplest form of grass skirt; from the elaborate local native court (Bose Levu), at which the great district chieftains are represented, to the all-embracing provincial parliament of the people (Bose vaka Turanga), where the ruling personages assemble.

Among these islands have occurred some of the most wonderful manifestations of the stupendous forces of nature ever witnessed by the eye of man, in the modification, alteration, and creation of land forms and in local disturbances of vast magnitude, through violent earthquakes or eruptive phenomena. Here, too, have occurred wide devastations and great destruction to property following the wake of periodical hurricanes along the equatorial belt.

These facts and many others come crowding to the mind when speaking of Polynesia, the South Sea Islands or their synonyms. While there is certainly no place on earth more beautiful, more enchanting, or more seductive to the island-dweller, there are few places where the forces of nature are more active, more varied, more constructive, or even more devastating.

A FIGHTING MAN OF AHIA, IN THE SOLOMON GROUP

It is not customary for the men of the Solomons to carry arms within their own villages, but they take this precautionary measure when wandering in forest or along shore. The favorite weapon is either a spear or an adze.

THE MARVEL OF THE CORAL REEF

Take, for example, the coral reef phenomenon by which islands are formed and connections established on a vast scale between widely separated areas, extending over thousands of miles of ocean. Also be it remembered that these immense submarine and subaërial coral masses, on which the very existence and stability of most of the Polynesian islands seem to depend, are the product of one of those low forms of animal life that enter so largely into

MEÑDANA, THE 16TH CENTURY SPANISH NAVIGATOR, CALLED THESE "THE ISLANDS OF SOLOMON" IN ANTICIPATION OF THEIR NATURAL RICHES

To the left may be seen an islet with a shrine to a dead chieftain (see illustration on page 8).

the economy of nature and make us feel that the combined efforts of men are comparatively feeble and ineffective.

Surely these remarkable coral formations are among the most truly wonderful evidences of lavish nature—mighty, far-reaching, and enduring.

There is nothing grander or more sublime than to be brought face to face with this ever-progressive and ever-expanding phenomenon—this vast, restless force, by which insular land-masses are formed and protected by encir-

cling reefs, the waters of the ocean held in check and the fury of the waves subdued.

It is one of the greatest wonders of nature, placed beyond the controlling influence of man, indestructible except by its own evolutionary power, but limited in range to the tropical waters of the globe. In the Pacific Ocean it attains its greatest development and on the Queensland coast it is strikingly represented by the Great Barrier Reef, extending for over a thousand miles along the shores to Torres Strait and far beyond.

THE SOLOMON ISLANDS METHOD OF "LAYING A GHOST"

The natives fear ghosts. If a chief has been powerful in life, it is believed his ghost will be powerful after his death. A shrine is made containing relics—the skull of the chief or his cremated body—and gifts of food are placed on near-by stones. It is taboo to pass behind the shrine.

SOLOMON ISLANDS VANITY

The ornaments of a South Sea islander are few and simple. He likes a necklace of beads or dog's teeth, or armlets made of plaited fiber or cut from single shells, and a crescent-shaped decoration of large pearly shell.

As a field for the marine biologist, the Great Barrier Reef, not yet fully explored, is of wide interest and has attracted attention in most of the scientific centers of the world, alluring to its fascinating waters representatives from both hemispheres of the globe.

A VOLCANIC BELT FROM JAPAN TO PERU

Then, again, we find in this vast oceanic region an immense volcanic influence, a great seismic belt extending from Japan to the Peruvian coast and including New Guinea and New Zealand.

In some of the island groups the volcanoes are still in a state of activity, and several years ago the Samoan Island of Savaii was for a time the scene of one of the greatest eruptions ever witnessed.

Most of the coralline islands of eastern Polynesia, extending on both sides of the Equator, bear traces of former volcanic activity, as evidenced by the numerous extinct craters scattered over the land-masses. That they have long been quiescent is clear from the dense vegetation everywhere covering the surface, except, perhaps, on the precipitous crater rims, where the sheer walls of rock afford little encouragement to plant life.

Few people realize that the Pacific Ocean covers more than a third part of the globe and contains within its vast periphery over half of the terrestrial water supply.

YOUNG STALWARTS OF THE SOLOMON ISLANDS

A TAMBU-HOUSE: SOLOMON ISLANDS

Toward the close of the day the front of the canoe-house is a rendezvous for the natives. Here they listen to and discuss the affairs of their world. A festival marks the completion of a new tambu-house, and formerly was accompanied by the sacrifice of a human life, the flesh being eaten and several of the bones used as decorations.

The influence exercised by this immense liquid surface on the climate and conditions of life in both hemispheres must be enormous, when we consider that it is bisected by the Equator and consequently exposed to the full force of the tropical sun. It is for this reason and because of the moist, equable temperature prevailing over the Polynesian region that we find in most of the oceanic islands great fertility of soil and a luxuriant vegetation, so that their rich natural resources afford ample provision for the inhabitants.

The early history of discovery in the "South Sea" goes away back to the days of Spanish maritime enterprise, in the beginning of the sixteenth century, when the Pacific Ocean was first seen by Balboa, on the 25th of September, 1513. Since then there have been many remarkable developments in the affairs of Polynesia, both in the occupation of the various groups of islands and in the life of the people.

MANY ISLAND GROUPS IN POLYNESIA

Geographically, the Polynesian region is occupied by numerous groups of islands of varying extent and importance, most of which are

DANCE FASHIONS IN NEW BRITAIN

The network that holds the leaves of a young coconut tree is as fine as India paper, very glossy, and of a beautiful silver color. Narrow strips of it are used as decorations by the natives in the "Kokomo" dance.

inhabited by a variety of peoples, generally known in Australia as Kanakas or South Sea Islanders.

Viewed in a broad and comprehensive light, this Polynesian Empire, if I may so call it, extends across the Pacific from the eastern waters of Australia and New Guinea for a hundred degrees of longitude to Easter Island. It includes the Bismarck Archipelago and Solomon group, New Caledonia and Fiji, the New Hebrides, Samoa, and Tonga, the Marshall and Caroline Islands, the Phoenix Group and Low Archipelago, the Hawaiian Islands, the Gilbert and Ellice Islands, the Society and Cook Islands, with numerous clusters of islands, reefs, and lagoons scattered over wide expanses of tropical ocean and studded like gems of emerald green on the vast coral sea that eternally surges along the equatorial belt of the great Pacific. Long regarded as the dream of early Spanish and Portuguese enterprise, these Polynesian islands have vast commercial possibilities.

MANY HARBORS OFFERING UNSURPASSED NAVAL BASES

Many of these Pacific groups possess beautiful harbors, commodious enough to shelter the largest ships of a major power. Most of them being guarded by impregnable barriers of coral reef, they would afford natural protection

A NEW BRITAIN NATIVE DANCE

Bodies which have been covered with oil and rubbed until they gleam and faces stained with red earth or berry juice present a weird picture to the island visitor. The women are not so fantastically dressed for the dance as the men, but they, too, are wearing their best "bibs and tuckers."

to all classes of shipping and could be utilized as naval bases of first-rate importance.

Commercially, the Pacific Island trade is a matter that will command world-wide attention in the affairs of national enterprise arising out of the World War. Profiting by her geographical position and the circumstances arising out of the war, Japan has made good use of her opportunities to occupy the Marshall Islands, over which she now holds a mandate, and in the struggle for a commercial footing in the Western Pacific she has shown herself a vigorous rival to British-Australian enterprise.

In physical structure these Polynesian islands are mostly composed of igneous or coralline rocks.

The moist southeast trade winds prevail over most of this region, the rainfall being generally high, especially in the eastern Solomons, about Bougainville Straits, 150 inches; Hawaii, 60 to 80 inches; New Caledonia, over 40 inches, and Suva, Fiji, 162 inches. On some of the low-lying atolls, however, the moisture-laden clouds pass over without any precipitation, and consequently there are occasionally narrow rainless zones, where accumulated deposits of guano occur, such as on Ocean and Nauru Islands (see pages 23 to 54). The rainy season usually lasts from November to April.

Although slightly relaxing, the climate on the whole is generally healthy, being free from endemic diseases, but malaria occurs on the

NEW GUINEA CHIEFS

Rigid plaited frames, or curved bands with a ground-
work of split cane, which support the cassowary or
paradise feather head ornaments, are made by the
men and worn at their dances. Necklaces consist
chiefly of various sorts of disk-like shells, either cut
or whole. Dancing aprons are made of bark cloth by
men and women, but colored by men only. The nose
rings are pencil-shaped pieces of shell about six inches long, which are passed through a hole in the nose.

low-lying areas in the Solomon and some other
large islands.

There is an oceanic flora in the coralline
groups, the prevailing forms being the coconut
and a few other palms, the pandanus and bread-
fruit tree. The edible roots are mostly represented by several varieties of the yam, the taro,
and sweet potato. On the larger groups of

islands, such as Fiji, the Hawaiian Archipelago,
the Solomons, and New Britain, there is a rich
forest vegetation mostly common to Australia
and New Guinea, although generally the
Papuan plants are more distinctively Asiatic in
character.

ANIMAL LIFE IS RESTRICTED

A remarkable feature of many of the Polynesian groups is the luxuriant vegetation on the
southeast, or windward, side of the islands, in
marked contrast to the northwest, or leeward,
side, where the forest is restricted to extremely
limited patches, with large reed-covered areas
of wide extent, suggesting aridity and the
absence of fertile soil. This is, no doubt, due to
the fact that a larger percentage of moisture is
deposited on the former, the prevailing southeast trade winds being comparatively dry by the
time they reach the opposite side.

In strange contrast to their luxuriant plant
life, the Pacific Islands cannot lay claim to a
rich fauna except in birds, which are fairly
numerous in New Caledonia, Fiji, and Hawaii.
The dog and the pig have a wide range, being
found everywhere within the influence of
native settlement, but both have been introduced in comparatively recent times and are
not indigenous to Polynesia.

There are several species of rodents and
some representatives of the bat family, which
appear to be the only indigenous mammals of
which we have any knowledge. Even insects
and reptiles are by no means plentiful, being
chiefly confined to small lizards, centipedes,
spiders, frogs, and harmless snakes.

In the Solomons the crocodile is met with,
both in fresh-water streams and tidal estuaries,
but here this saurian reaches its easternmost

A HAVEN OF REST: NEW GUINEA

With the yam, taro, and banana available, it is difficult to convince the Papuan that he should work for wages, for which he has no use.

limit, as it occurs nowhere else in the island groups beyond.

From this brief description of the physical and climatic conditions of the Pacific islands, it must be clear that no place could be more ideal for the abode of man than this great and enchanting oceanic region, this seductive "Insulandia," midst reef and palm, perpetual sunshine, and evergreen verdure, the dream of romantic youth, the home of early buccaneering enterprise, and

the scene of great human struggles in tribal warfare, when the cannibal feast was deemed a fitting celebration of victory on the field of battle.

Some attention must now be given to the aboriginal inhabitants of Oceanica. Ethnologically considered, they naturally belong to two distinct classes or divisions of the human family, beginning first of all with the Polynesians, comprising the Maoris, Samoans, Fijians, and Tongans, whose racial affinities are still in dispute. In physical characteristics they are roundheaded, narrow-nosed, of a light-brown color, with round orbits and lank, black hair. They are also generally tall in stature.

On the other hand, the second division, known to ethnologists as Melanesians, are long-headed, broad-nosed, of a black color, with low orbits, black, frizzly hair, and are comparatively short of stature.

In the primitive state the Melanesians are considered savage and not infrequently treacherous, in contrast to the Polynesians, who, on the other hand, are believed to be more concerned with public appearance, even gaining positions in the public service in New Zealand and in Hawaii.

But even the Melanesians of the present, with the exception of those comparatively few natives living in remote and isolated inland villages, are not the same sort as those met with in the early days of missionary enterprise, when pioneering intercourse was not always attended with freedom from danger to the trader, recruiter of labor, or planter. Now it is an easy matter to land on any of the islands and do business with the natives without risk of hostile attack. The Polynesian of today is in point of fact a keen trader and fully alive to the advantages of doing business with westerners.

PEOPLED BY PHŒNICIANS?

As to the origin of these Pacific islanders, opinions differ, it being held by some authorities that they have been allied to various races, including the Aryans, the American aborigines, and the Papuans.

In the writer's view, there can be no doubt that the islands of Polynesia were originally peopled by Phœnicians, whose migratory influence extended to the coast of Peru. This theory is strongly supported by the presence of the numerous cyclopean monuments, huge monolithic statues, paved avenues, and ramparts of walls of basaltic blocks over thirty feet in length, brought from great distances, on Easter Island and in the Carolines. It is evident that none of the present races could erect such immense structures as these (see pages 66 and 68).

The subject is fascinating and could be further elucidated to any extent, under circumstances appropriate to its discussion.

MYSTERIOUS RUINS ON EASTER ISLAND

The remarkable ruins of ancient settlement in the Caroline Islands are one of the mysteries of Polynesia and will probably never be solved. When it is considered that some of the stones forming the walls of those extensive ruins are of immense size and are supposed to have been brought from other islands of the group across storm-tossed channels and placed in their present position with precision and masterly skill, it is apparent that all this could not have been done by people akin to the present inhabitants, but must have been the handiwork of skilled craftsmen similar to the builders of the ancient ruins in Peru and Mexico and perhaps, also, Africa.

If this view be accepted as reasonably sound, we may assume that Polynesia was formerly the home of a civilization that has long since disappeared and become extinct, leaving imperishable monuments of skilled craftsmanship on Easter Island and the Carolines, or else the islanders are a decadent people.

Be this as it may, the fact remains that these ruins are a mystery to the present inhabitants of the Pacific islands, who typically have no knowledge of the art of building in stone.

Even native tradition is singularly silent as to the origin of the inhabitants and their migratory movements among the island groups.

THE FATE OF THE
EARLY INHABITANTS:
AN UNSOLVED PROBLEM

As to the fate of the original prehistoric inhabitants, who left such indelible traces of a higher order of civilization behind them as exists in the cyclopean ruins of the Carolines, we have no means of knowing, and mere conjecture can help but little. Whether they were over-whelmed by some mighty and widespread cataclysm or exterminated by epidemic disease will probably never be known.

Is it possible these ruins may have had their origin in some migratory wave sweeping across the Pacific from the shores of Asia to the coast of South America? Had this been the case we should expect to find some marked traces of Asiatic blood in the present inhabitants; but instead of this the dark Melanesians bear greater resemblance to the Papuans, while, next to the Patagonians, the Polynesians are the tallest people on the globe and are allied to the Maoris of New Zealand.

The only feature in which they bear any resemblance to the peoples of Eastern countries is in the practice of circumcision, and this is not general, but mostly confined to the Western Pacific.

In point of fact, there is stronger ground for assuming that the Polynesian peoples are remotely allied to the Australian aborigines, on account of the ceremony of initiation of youths into the rites of manhood which is practiced by both. In Australia this is known as the "Bora" ceremony, and in the Fiji group it is called the "Nanga," both having the same significance and purpose, with only slight variations in the mode of procedure, as clearly established by the late Rev. Lorimer Fison in collaboration with the writer, whose investigations extended over several years.

PHOSPHATES IN LIEU OF
MINERAL WEALTH

In natural resources these Pacific islands differ to some extent from Australia, New Zealand, and New Guinea, there being, so far as is known, an absence of great and rich mineral deposits; but the soils are extremely rich, and for the production of sugar, cotton, rubber, coconuts, bananas, coffee, cocoa, rice, pineapples, and many varieties of fruit and vegetables they are eminently suitable and probably unsurpassed. It would indeed be difficult to name any product of tropical origin that could not flourish in the fertile soils of Polynesia.

Among the greatest of all the natural resources of these oceanic territories the enormous deposits of high-grade phosphates on several of the Polynesian islands are of prime importance. This is especially so in the case of Nauru, or Pleasant Island, a small, isolated spot half a degree south of the Equator and rising about twenty feet above sea-level. It is estimated by Dr. Paul Hombrun to contain about 497,700,000 tons of the richest phosphates to be obtained anywhere, the quantitative analysis giving from 83 to 90 per cent of tricalcium phosphate (see page 30).

Although this remarkable little isle has no harbor, the phosphates are loaded into the freighters at the rate of 100 tons per hour by special contrivances. The Ocean Island high-grade phosphate deposits are estimated at 12,500,000 tons.

MURAL ART IN NEW GUINEA

There are also rich phosphate deposits on the islands of Angaur, in the Pelew group, and Makatea, the estimated quantity on the latter—an island belonging to France, on the western side of the Tuamotu or Low Archipelago—being 10,000,000 tons.

PACIFIC ISLANDS DISTRIBUTED AMONG MANY NATIONS

Before the World War the Nauru and Angaur deposits were in German hands. This suggests some brief consideration of the political or pre-war condition of these Pacific groups, especially in the light of their occupation by European powers and their present relation to the Australian continent and to New Zealand.

At the outbreak of the World War the Pacific islands were in the possession of the United States of America, Great Britain, France,* and Germany. Japan at that time had but small interests, as occupant of the Bonin (Ogasawara) Islands, a small group of about 38 square miles in extent.

In area and population the United States possessions certainly rank first in importance, the comparatively large territories of the Philippines and the Hawaiian Islands, with American Samoa and Guam, giving that country premier place among the great powers interested in the Pacific.

The possessions formerly held by Germany in the Pacific were: Kaiser Wilhelm's Land—area, 70,135 square miles, population, 110,000; Bismarck Archipelago and a part of the Solomon group—area, 22,046 square miles, population, 210,000; Caroline Islands—area, 598 square miles, population, 30,900; Mariana Islands—area, 241 square miles, population, 1,118 (exclusive of Guam); Marshall Islands—area, 156 square miles, population, 10,000; German Samoa—area, 933 square miles, population, 37,000.

*For an account of the Marquesas Islands, owned by France, see "A Vanishing People of the South Seas," by John W. Church, in the October, 1919, number of the NATIONAL GEOGRAPHIC MAGAZINE

SUCH CASCADES AS THIS ON THE PACHU RIVER, IN CHOISEUL, SERVE TO
JUSTIFY THE USE OF THE PHRASE "SCENIC PARADISE," SO OFTEN APPLIED
TO THE ISLANDS OF THE PACIFIC

TYPICAL SAMOANS

The lightest of their race in color, the Samoans are true Polynesians, prepossessing in appearance and manner, and of splendid physique. The men treat their women with great respect and kindness and lavish affection upon their children. They are scrupulously clean, bathing at least twice a day.

It will thus be seen that, with widely scattered territories aggregating 94,169 square miles, stretching diagonally across the Pacific from Samoa on the southeast to the Mariana Islands on the northwest, for a distance of over 3,300 miles and parallel to the seaboard of northeast Australia, Germany held the key to the Western Pacific.

ISLANDS SUITABLE FOR NAVAL BASES

On each of these groups enumerated a naval base could be established and its posi-tion rendered secure against attack by suitable fortifications and the natural advantages afforded by the coral-reef structures.

Once this was done, a hostile power would be in a position practically to dominate the whole of the Pacific Ocean. With submarines and a fleet of destroyers, it would be a simple matter to isolate Australia and New Zealand, as the enormous oil supply of Sumatra, the coals of Australia, and the inexhaustible food resources of the Pacific islands would obviate the necessity of leaving the locality for supplies of any kind. And from such a position it would be equally effective in

THE GRAVE OF ROBERT LOUIS STEVENSON, ON OPOLU, SAMOAN ISLANDS

On the summit of Mount Vaea a cemented monument, in accordance with native design, has been erected, by native labor, over the grave of Robert Louis Stevenson. On the side facing the east are carved his own words:

> "Under the wide and starry sky,
> Dig the grave and let me lie,
> Glad did I live and gladly die;
>   And I laid me down with a will."

> "This be the verse you grave for me:
> Here he lies where he longed to be;
> Home is the sailor, home from sea,
>   And the hunter home from the hill."

Chiseled on the tomb are a thistle and a hibiscus flower, typical of his countries.

blocking the Panama Canal, in interrupting communication across the Indian Ocean, invading the East Indies, the Philippines, and menacing Japan.

CONTROL OF THE ISLANDS REDISTRIBUTED

In point of fact, there is no other region on the globe possessing such remarkable natural facilities for the dominating purposes of an ambitious and aggressive power.

As an outcome of the defeat of the Central Powers and the distribution at Paris of the control of enemy colonial possessions, the Australian Mandate gives to that commonwealth complete control over Germany's former Pacific territories, with the exception of Samoa, the Marshall, Caroline, and Mariana Islands, and the phosphate deposits of Nauru, the ownership of the last named being shared with Great Britain and New Zealand.

German Samoa was placed under a New Zealand mandate.

The Japanese hold the Marshall, the Mariana (except Guam), and the Caroline Islands under the Peace Conference mandate, and have lost no time in getting a firm footing, not only there, but in other groups of the Pacific, for the purpose of trade.

There is a monthly service of steamers between Japan and the Marshall Islands, and Japanese goods are being distributed among the islanders in all the groups of the Pacific.

NAURU, THE RICHEST ISLAND IN THE SOUTH SEAS

By Rosamond Dodson Rhone

THE mandates for the Pacific islands which formerly belonged to Germany were assigned to the powers who seized them in the first year of the war: to Japan, the German islands north of the Equator; to New Zealand, German Samoa; to Australia, German New Guinea, the German Solomons; to Great Britain, the island of Nauru. There have been doubts expressed as to whether these mandates are not proving to their holders more of a burden than an asset, but Nauru is probably the richest spot on the globe for its size.

This is a story of the island whose name has risen to notice in the new geographies, as a by-product of the upheaval caused by the World War, just as, owing to some geological upheaval ages ago, the island itself arose from the sea.

GERMANY CAME LATE INTO THE PACIFIC

This story of Nauru under white control is the story of German possessions in the South Seas. Germany came late into the Pacific; all the good things had been taken. The explorers—Dutch, British, French, and Spanish—had pretty well divided up the islands, for in their day "findings were keepings."

The German colonial policy was undertaken in 1883 by financing certain chartered companies which had been trading with the islands for about 25 years. By this means Germany acquired a protectorate over a part of northern New Guinea. A protectorate is the camel's nose in the tent. When he gets his head in and his hump, it becomes a colony.

New Guinea is shaped like a dragon, with a Dutch head and shoulders, British underparts and tail, and German back and rump. Perhaps, from the German colonial point of view, their portion was the saddle, in which they would override the entire Pacific.

In 1886 an agreement between Great Britain and Germany, defining the "Limit of spheres of influence in the Western Pacific," was signed at Berlin. This was the camel's head and hump. By this all lands unappropriated by other powers were divided between the two contracting parties. It was something like the division of the earth between Abram and Lot— one took the East and the other the West. In this case Great Britain took the East and Germany the West.

The language of the deed is not like the language of deeds of land; there are no corners and boundaries of adjacent properties; no "lands, tenements, and hereditaments"; but the terminology of navigation is drawn upon to furnish the descriptions.

The division line starts on land, but at once puts out to sea. It begins at a point on the northeast coast of New Guinea on the boundary line between British and German territory, thence east along a parallel of latitude to a point in the Pacific Ocean marked on a British admiralty chart, thence from point to point on admiralty charts to a point fifteen degrees north latitude and 173° 30' east longitude.

GERMANY PURCHASED ISLANDS FROM SPAIN

This line of cleavage gave to Germany the Marshall group, a large number of islands north of New Guinea, rechristened the Bismarck Archipelago, some of the Solomon Islands, and a small coral island almost under the Equator, which is Nauru.

Three years later Germany added to her Pacific holdings by buying from Spain the Caroline group west of the Marshalls, and the Ladrones, with the exception of Guam, which had been previously acquired by the United States as a by-product of the Spanish-American War.

About the same time, she acquired by agreement with Great Britain and America (ceding to the former part of the Solomon group) two islands in the Samoan group, one of which was the last home of Robert Louis Stevenson and on whose summit is his tomb (see page 21).

In this way Germany acquired her island possessions; she held them for about thirty years; we all know how she lost them.

When Germany took possession of the islands she made Jaluit the seat of government for the Marshalls and assigned Nauru to that group, although it was an island altogether *on its own*, as the British say, having its own language and customs and lying 300 miles distant. There is no physical likeness, as it is an upheaved coral island, while the Marshalls are low-lying atolls.

AT THE "JUMPING-OFF PLACE" OF THE WORLD

Nauru, or Pleasant Island, is almost at the jumping-off place of the world; it is not exactly "East of the sun and west of the moon," but it is almost the farthest east, being only thirteen degrees west of the international date line, and it is a half degree south of the Equator. It is one of the *Line* islands.

Before it fell to Germany it knew no white rulers, but was governed by its own immemorial laws, enforced by its own chiefs; but white influence had impinged upon it for many years. Whaling ships from New England ports called there and traded firearms for drinking coconuts and island pigs. It was rather a poor island in those far-off days, before its great wealth was discovered. It had no sandalwood or tortoise shell; no pearls or *bêche-de-mer*; not even copra, for copra was not made in the Pacific before 1872 and coconut oil was not an article of commerce.

There are on Nauru two monuments to contact with American whalers. One is of flesh and blood—a native family whose curly hair is

OBVIATING THE DIFFICULTY OF HARBOR NAVIGATION AT NAURU

Because of the coral reef, which slopes beneath the sea at an angle of 45 degrees off Nauru, the phosphate company has provided deep-sea moorings. Large buoys lie on the surface of the sea at a safe distance outside the edge of the reef, while small ones are lined close to it. A motor launch operated by a native engineer is seen leaving the small-boat harbor and crossing the reef through the surf at high tide (see text, page 36).

in striking contrast to their straight-haired neighbors, witnessing that the ancestor was a runaway black sailor. The other is a small cannon, which stands before the house of the British administrator.

THE ISLANDERS' REVENGE

In the fifties, a whaling ship out of New Bedford, Massachusetts, called at the island, and the natives paddled out in their outrigger canoes and swarmed over the decks, examining everything with lively curiosity. They especially admired a small cannon, whose polished brass glittered in the tropic sunshine, and they offered to buy it, paying for it with coconuts. A price was agreed upon. They went ashore and returned with the required number, but the captain raised the price, asking double the number.

The natives again went ashore and brought back the stipulated number; the captain again raised the price. It was now late in the day and the natives said they would bring the remainder in the morning. They beached their canoes and retired to their huts, while the crew, drinking the delicious coconut milk and feasting on the delicate meat, no doubt felicitated themselves, as the ship drifted about waiting for the dawn, on their cleverness in outwitting the simple savages.

NAURU ARCHITECTURE

The houses built on piles are usually smaller than those built on the ground. The former, about 22 feet in length and 15 feet in width, are supported on a framework of stout poles fastened to the top of the piles by broad strips of rattan. The ground houses average 30 feet in length by 20 feet in width.

In the night the natives went out in force, surprised and overcame the officers and crew, and killed every man save one sailor who secreted himself. They set fire to the ship and took the cannon; they took nothing else!

Other white influences were traders who took native wives, and the traditional "beachcombers"—runaway sailors, sometimes escaped convicts, and white men "gone native," who lived in native huts upon native food.

There were also more benign influences. French Catholic missions and English and American Protestant ones were established. The island became nominally Christian, but without abandoning the combats between the tribes.

The Nauruans have never been cannibals, but they had the reputation of being savage warriors. A traveler from New Zealand—not Macaulay's New Zealander standing on a broken arch of London Bridge—who visited the island just before the Germans took possession, found the natives all armed and involved in deadly feuds. He counted nine kinds of rifles of English and American make, besides several cannon. There were then ten white traders living near each other along the beach and some of their half-caste descendants are there today.

When Germany took over the islands she gave the natives a certain number of days to give up their arms. They generally obeyed, but a few threw theirs into the caves which underlie the island, where they are found from time to time by exploring parties.

GOOD ROADS CREDITED TO GERMANY

The Germans are credited with building roads and they also taught the natives to make copra.

The native method of making coconut oil was to rely upon the sun's heat to extract it from the broken up or shredded meats, and to finish the process by putting the shredded coconut into a bag made of the canvas-like stipules of the coconut leaf and placing it under a clumsy press which was merely a timber, one end of which was thrust into a notch in a tree trunk, while upon the free end the weight of several persons was thrown.

This was more work than which the South Sea islander was accustomed. He has made coconut oil for his own use in this manner from the time "when the memory of man runneth not to the contrary," but he could not be persuaded to make it commercially.

Copra is easily made and stored. The meat of the ripe coconut is broken into pieces and dried in the sun just long enough to extract the moisture; then it is bagged and ready for sale.

In the South Seas copra is a magic word. For this the Pacific trader dares the malaria and savages of the Solomons and the New Hebrides, and the teeth of the coral reefs. The trade store and copra shed stand on the beach of every coral isle, and when a steamer or schooner calls, the surf-boats go in and out, over the reef at high tide or through intricate channels when there is an open lagoon, carrying trade goods and returning with bags of copra.

The Germans promulgated laws, the chiefs being held responsible for their enforcement. Taxes were imposed—head tax, dog tax, and bicycle tax—and the men were required to work on the roads three days of each week.

THE STORY OF THE DISCOVERY OF PHOSPHATE

The colonial government did not know what a treasure they had under their feet, but were content to run a little trade store, a branch of the Jaluit store, which sold to the natives tobacco and beer, Alaska canned salmon, sugar,

A PHOSPHATE TRAMWAY

This electric tram line is used to haul phosphate to the piers, where it is shot into the surf-boats to be carried to the cargo vessel. In Australia, where some 200,000 tons of this fertilizer are used each year, phosphate has doubled the wheat crop.

rice, and ship biscuits in exchange for copra. They also sold prints and thin Japanese silks for the Mother Hubbard dresses which the American missionaries taught the native women to wear and for the lava-lavas which the native men wore to the mission churches.

Then came a great change, owing to the discovery of phosphate.

One day Nauru, like Aphrodite, arose dripping from the sea. The date of this emergence cannot be more nearly indicated than *ages ago*, and the term *day* is not limited to twenty-four hours, but is to be construed liberally, like the *days* of Genesis. The island may indeed have been thrust suddenly into the air, with all her lovely polyps gasping and shriveling in the tropic sun, and scarlet fishes and long-armed octopi leaping affrighted out of the exposed caves to the safe shelter of the sea, while slow-moving sea-urchins and mollusks perished in the potholes and labyrinths of the coral; or the process of elevation may have been gradual, life in the coral dying gradually at the emerged top, while it remained in full vigor just beneath the level of low tide.

At any rate, when the upheaval was complete, when the fairy towers and pinnacles and the unsunned caverns of the sea had been lifted into the blaze of the sun, life at its base beneath

COÖPERATION IN CANOE-MAKING

All the men turn out on Nauru for canoe-making. The felled tree is dragged to the beach, where it is trimmed and barked, to the accompaniment of shouting and singing. It is floated to the village and beached; then the experienced canoe-maker hollows and shapes it with a stone adze.

the sea continued unabated and the fringing reef was slowly extended around it.

At this period the island must have looked like those fantastic artificial structures which we see in aquariums. No product of man's construction could be more extravagant in conception than these pinnacles, towers, bridges, flying buttresses, their shapes always suggesting architectural fantasies upreared into the air. There it stood, bare and bald as did the earth on that day in Genesis when the dry land first appeared.

THE SEA-BIRDS BRING WEALTH

Then came the sea-birds, millions and millions of them, feeding on the abundant sea-food, nesting in the coral, hatching their young in ever-increasing multitudes, and depositing the waste of their bodies in the coral till the lower crevices were filled and a gradually rising body of guano attained at length a level with the tops of the pinnacles, and then rose above them and lay in a level plateau across the island.*

On the margin the rains, the winds, and the breakers, spouting high against the coral, washed away this deposit, so that ramparts of bare pinnacles stood up and still stand all around the island; but the coral walls back from the shore held safe the treasure. Came another

*See also, "Peru's Wealth-Producing Birds," by R. E. Coker, in the NATIONAL GEOGRAPHIC MAGAZINE for June, 1920.

SOLVING THE SHIP-TONNAGE PROBLEM IN NAURU

In the building of an outrigger canoe, one man is in charge and does most of the work, but timber for the outrigger and platforms must be provided by his assistants. Coconut sennit is used to fasten the timbers together. The woman in the background is holding a roll of pandanus strips used in basket-making and in weaving mats such as the ones in the foreground. The latter constitute the "weather boarding" for native houses.

day (I am aware that I am flinging *days* about as casually as the author of Genesis). The sea-birds were gone; not a keen red eye or swift-diving wing was left; gone, immemorially gone. How or why is a mystery.

Then in the alembic of Nature a transformation occurred. Guano is chiefly phosphoric acid and nitrogen; coral is chiefly lime. Somehow, by the close contact, the guano became changed into phosphate of lime, which is guano raised to the nth power. It had now become a hard rock, odorless and generally colorless, although some specimens show fine, dark stratification and take a high polish.

Another day—perhaps the same day—(it is startling to see how closely this follows the Genesis story of creation)—vegetation appeared, narrowly limited in species, but abundant in specimens; and finally man, the people of the South Sea. This must have been the order, for where there is no vegetation there is no population.

The vegetation owed nothing to the wealth of phosphate beneath it. Phosphate is not soluble in water. It needs treatment with sulphuric acid, which converts it into super-phosphate to let loose its treasure of stimulation for plants.

East of Nauru, 160 miles, lies Ocean Island, or Banaba, another island the story of whose origin is Nauru's story. Like twin sisters they stand unrelated to their nearest neigh-

THE TACKLE OF THE SWAMP FISHER OF THE SOUTH PACIFIC

Rattan is used in the making of these fish traps. They are five or more feet high and are set in swamps, especially in New Guinea. The fisherman roasts his catch in a covering of cane and bamboo.

bors, the low-lying atolls, their only relative being the island of Makatea in the Tuamotu group (Paumotos), more than 2,000 miles distant, where the evolution of phosphate followed the same lines.

A DISCARDED DOOR-STOP PROVES CLUE TO FABULOUS WEALTH

A few years ago the Pacific Islands Company had schooners cruising in the Pacific for various tropical products, especially guano, which was growing so scarce that they were "brooming" it from tiny coral islands. One of the captains brought from Ocean Island to the Sydney office of the company a piece of curious stratified rock with the suggestion that it might be made into children's marbles. This rock remained knocking around the office for years, being used as a door-stop. Finally the manager of the company analyzed it and found to his amazement that it was 80 per cent phosphate of lime. He boarded the next schooner sailing for Ocean Island, which had fallen upon the eastern side of the line of demarkation and so became British territory.

The Pacific Islands Company was reorganized as the Pacific Phosphate Company. The British Colonial Government granted permission to buy land of the natives for opening quarries and building a plant with crushers, loading bins, and tramways, and before the war interfered with the shipping the annual output was 100,000 tons, worth when loaded on the ships $12.50 per ton.

As soon as the phosphate works were established upon Ocean Island, the company extended its operations to Nauru. Application was made to the German Government for a concession, which was granted on condition that the Germans were taken into partnership. A fine plant was built on the lines of that at Ocean Island. There was a British manager and a German manager, each with his own staff.

A white settlement was built, the Germans bringing knock-down houses from Germany, which were set up in rows and named "Berlin," "Stuttgart," "Cologne," while the British houses were named for British and colonial cities. Each house had a garden of flowers, the walks edged with white coral; in the German gardens the walks were bordered with inverted beer bottles.

A German governor was sent to the island. A two-story house was built for him (the only one on Nauru) and a full-length portrait of the Kaiser hung on its wall. The grounds were planted with beautiful tropical trees and shrubs, and the flag with the two-headed eagle was hoisted on a tall pole on the beach.

On the hilltop was erected one of those fine wireless stations which Germany placed at each of her strategic points in the Pacific. This was a triangular mast of structural steel 420 feet high, resting upon glass disks and guyed to massive concrete pillars. *Then came the war!* How many stories of fact and fiction contain these words—*then came the war.*

"UNDER TWO FLAGS"

After the Australian navy had put an end to the spectacular career of the *Emden*, it reached out to strike the enemy in other places. German New Guinea was captured, and then a warship was sent to Nauru. The flag of the two-headed eagle was hauled down and the flag of the Crosses of Saint George, Saint Andrew, and Saint Patrick was hoisted. The German residents agreed to submit to British control. Then the warship steamed away. It was no sooner out of sight than the Germans, who had thrown their arms and ammunition over the reef upon her first appearance, broke their parole and hoisted their flag.

The next day a Japanese man-of-war, fresh from conquest of the Carolines and Ladrones, was sighted by the lookout on top of the wireless mast. The British flag was again hoisted and the warship steamed past without calling. A few days later the British flag was burned in a spectacular manner on the sports ground, after which the governor ordered all British subjects to go aboard a small cargo ship for deportation to Ocean Island.

These exiles, including women and children, about forty in number, reached Ocean Island the next day and were assigned homes with the company staff there. Ocean Island had no wireless at that time, so it was two months before the news could be sent to Rabaul, in New Guinea, the nearest point of military occupation, and measures taken to turn the tables upon the Germans.

A ship was sent, with officers and soldiers and a machine-gun. It called first at Ocean Island and took on board the deportees, who were carried back to Nauru. The Germans were arrested and deported to Sydney, where they were interned during the war and then

AN ILLUSTRATED FISH STORY

The most popular forms of fishing paraphernalia used on the island of Nauru are bows and arrows and spears. This catch of brilliantly colored fish seems to be a satisfactory one. The tree in the background is a banyan.

sent to Germany. Their native wives and half-caste children remained on Nauru.

An Australian garrison was left, pending the duration of the war. A British administrator took the place of the German governor, and King George the Fifth looks down from the wall today where Kaiser Wilhelm used to scowl behind his mustache.

A DOG REVEALS HIDDEN RADIO EQUIPMENT

An Australian wireless staff took over the plant on the hilltop and adopted a little dog left over from the German occupation. Whenever the members approached a certain pile of coral blocks on the rocky hill near the station the dog became excited, barking and attempting to dig, as if something were hidden beneath it. Upon investigation they uncovered the mouth of a natural shaft in the coral, at the foot of which caves opened. In one of these they discovered a quantity of material belonging to the wireless plant, which had been secreted by the Germans. The dog was named "Radio."

The German impress on the South Seas is not great. They left some fine wireless stations, some fine government residences, some

A NAURU "TOPER"

After the coconut has attained full size, and long before it is ripe, it contains a pint or more of delicious juice, called in the different languages of the islands, wine, water, or milk, and what could be more refreshing in the blistering heat of the tropics than this cool drink, with its bit of a tang!

botanical gardens; they left good roads. They left no colonies to speak of and their language made no impression.

One New Guinea governor stated that if during his tenure of office he was successful in teaching the natives to speak good German instead of English he would be doing good work, but this failed and all officials were obliged to give orders in pidgin English.

The German flag which was hauled down on Nauru was shown to me at Ocean Island spread out upon the veranda of the British residency by the commissioner of the Gilbert and Ellice Colony, to which the island belongs. He said (this was during the war): "I wonder if this flag will ever again float in the Pacific."

NAURU UNDER BRITISH CONTROL

Nauru has about twelve hundred natives. Early in 1918 the chiefs, who had been under German rule for twenty-eight years before the war and under British rule pending the war, came to the administrator and asked him to send a petition to King George the Fifth to keep the island and not let it be returned to Germany.

The administrator thereupon summoned all the natives, men and women, to appear before him and declare themselves British or German subjects. This was the first plebiscite growing out of the war, and it took place in what was perhaps the most remote territory in the world. It suggested that day in the Old Testament when Joshua called all the tribes of Israel to Shechem and said to them: "Choose you this day whom ye will serve!"

This was a great day for Nauru. Perhaps the crowd that gathered in Shechem on that far-off day was no more picturesque in appearance than those who came together on this little coral island.

The men of the Solomon Islands are particularly fond of wearing the brilliantly colored hibiscus in their hair.

As upon a festal day, the natives crowned themselves with fresh wreaths of flowers, and those who were nearest to the white settlement or under missionary influence put on "plenty clothes," the men wearing clean lava-lavas falling to the knee and the women Mother Hubbard dresses reaching to their bare heels, while those from more remote parts of the island, or avowedly pagan, came dressed only in *ridis* of pandanus leaves, swinging from their hips like ballet dancers' skirts, their bare brown torsos glistening with coconut oil.

They came on foot, on bicycles—a native in a *ridi*, riding a bicycle is a delightful anachronism,—some of the aged and feeble were drawn in light carts by man (or woman) power. Perhaps the most picturesque figure in that company was an old man named Tekoroa, dressed in a mat wrapped about his waist and reaching to his knees, encasing him tightly, like an envelope. Before there was a white government he killed seven men, natives, cast upon the beach by the waves, in order to seize their canoe.

They assembled at the government courthouse, which is built like a native house, a high, wide shed supported by posts of coconut timbers, roofed by a deeply caved thatch of pandanus leaves and floored by coarse coconut mats. Guided by the native police, they passed in line before the administrator's desk and subscribed themselves without exception, British subjects. They can all read and write in their own language, for the missionaries have spread education throughout the islands.

MINING AND SHIPPING OF PHOSPHATE

Phosphate is mined by Chinese coolies in open quarries, but these are not like stone quarries, where everything is taken out as the work progresses. The phosphate is packed between the coral pinnacles as tightly as the filling in a tooth and must be excavated, leaving the pinnacles standing.

There is, perhaps, no hotter working place on earth, for as the workmen descend, digging and blasting, they are below the level of the trade wind's cool breath and exposed to the fierce rays of the tropic sun.

When a coolie has filled a pair of baskets he hangs one on each end of a carrying-pole and makes his way by devious paths through the worked-out places to a central carrier, called the "flying fox," running on a cable. He dumps his baskets and trots back for another load, while the carrier conveys the phosphate to a hopper, a tall wooden tower with chutes, from which it is dropped into cars ready to take it to the dryers, huge buildings containing crushing and drying machinery and storage bins for the finished product.

A worked-out phosphate field is a dismal, ghastly tract of land, with its thousands of upstanding white coral pinnacles from ten to thirty feet high, its cavernous depths littered with broken coral, abandoned tram tracks, discarded phosphate baskets, and rusted American kerosene tins. Yet, in this waste, vegetation begins and young pandanus trees and sprouting coconuts are opening vigorous leaves and sending strong roots downward into the crevices of the coral.

To get an adequate idea of the expense and difficulty of equipping and maintaining the phosphate works, which include the maintenance of the employees, one must understand that the islands furnish nothing except coral rock and sand for rock and concrete foundations, and a little fruit and an abundance of fish for food. On Ocean Island even the use of sand is prohibited by the government, as there is very little sandy beach, the island being edged by vertical cliffs of coral. With this exception, whatever I say of Nauru is equally true of Ocean Island.

Even fresh water is lacking and must be provided by catchment areas for rainwater, the iron roofs of buildings serving this purpose, with galvanized iron tanks and concrete cisterns for storage, while sea water is used in the sewerage system and for the fire department. In case of lack of rainfall, and the Line islands are subject to severe droughts, fresh water is furnished by condensing sea water.

NO HARBOR IN NAURU

Every bit of wood, steel and brick for building and furnishing, every piece of machinery, all articles of clothing and food, are brought over 2,000 miles in ships from Australia. To the ordinary hazards of ocean cargoes is added the difficulty of unloading from rolling ships into tossing surf-boats. Sometimes the stevedore's gang misses the boat and drops a bulky piece of cargo, such as a piano, into the sea, when, even if it is salvaged, it retains a salt-sea tang on its wires.

There are low islands, atolls, that have practically no leeward side, but are all windward—that is, the winds blow right over them, and the sea on all sides is agitated so violently that it is not possible to land anywhere on their shores; there are others which have lagoons with one side open to the sea, through which ships can pass into safe harbors.

Nauru has no harbor, no anchorage, but she has a leeward shore, the western side, where, for the greater part of the year, ships can lie "off and on" sheltered by the bulk of the island from the winds which beat incessantly upon the windward side.

Formerly ships were obliged to lie "off and on," and some of them came too far *on* and were wrecked on the reef, but now there are deep-sea moorings provided by the phosphate company. Huge buoys lie on the surface of the sea, at a safe distance outside the edge of the reef, anchored far down beneath the surface and attached to the reef by "bridles"—chains bolted to the surface of the reef. The reef does not break off abruptly, but slopes beneath the sea at an angle of 45 degrees, so that 100 yards from the shore the water is 100 yards deep.

With infinite toil and patience these moorings are laid, as the mooring ship can work only in reasonably calm weather, and as soon as they are complete the sea endeavors to

TEACHERS AND PUPILS OF A MISSIONARY NATIVE SCHOOL

tear them loose. "White horses" is not a far-fetched figure of speech for the crests forever hurdling the deep-green waves. Like wild stallions bitted and bridled, they tear at the steel "bridles" of the moorings and lash out with thrashing heels at the buoys, while beneath the surface the steel cables are gnawed by salt water, and polyps load them with their fairy palaces of living coral.

When all the difficulties of mining, crushing, and drying the phosphate have been overcome and the loaded cars have been run out upon the piers ready to shoot their loads into surf-boats, there may come a "westerly"—that is, the wind may change and blow toward the shore. Then the ships, which always have steam up and watches kept, as if at sea, loose their moorings and go out to sea, where they drift about, waiting for the wind to change.

One ship made a record by drifting for three months while waiting a chance to take on cargo, coming up to the island daily to signal. At length she ran out of coal and a collier came up from Sydney to supply her, but as it was impossible to tranship the coal on account of the violence of the sea, the ship, with the attendant collier, proceeded to a lagoon in the Carolines, where she filled her bunkers.

LABOR RECRUITED FROM DISTANT ISLANDS

The two classes of laborers, the workers in the phosphate field and the loading crews on the cars and boats, include few natives of Nauru. The former, as we have seen, are Chinese coolies, the latter Kanakas recruited from other islands. A Kanaka is a South Sea islander.

THIS IS THE LIFE IN NAURU

Not the least of this island's attractions are the many beautiful lagoons into which coral rock pinnacles and coconut palms throw sharp reflections.

The word is a general term meaning *man*; but no islander applies it to himself or to men of his own island. He uses it as a tern of contempt.

Every two or three years a ship is sent among the Marshalls, Carolines, and Gilbert and Ellice groups to recruit laborers and to return the Kanakas whose terms have expired.

The recruited laborer hires himself to the "company" not on account of wages, but as a chance to travel, to see the world. He is assured of food and shelter and, if he has a wife and family, is given married quarters. He looks upon the wage as "velvet," to be spent on such luxuries as gay lava-lavas made in Manchester, England; for tobacco, sugar, canned salmon, jewsharps, and accordions.

He takes life lightly, hilariously, and gets much amusement out of his employment. Not for him the arduous labor of the phosphate field—none will undertake that but the plodding worker—but the rush and roar of the steam and trolley phosphate trains, the pitching and tossing of the surf-boats under the end of the cantilever, whose long steel arm reaches beyond the edge of the reef, as the phosphate is shot down through a flexible canvas chute into huge baskets, amid clouds of dust, usually reaching its objective, but sometimes spilling into the sea to the accompaniment of shouts and laughter.

With singing, shouting, yelling, the string of surf-boats is pulled by a motor launch out to

BUADA LAGOON, SHELTERED BY ONE OF NAURU'S COCONUT GROVES

The fish-pond partition in this lagoon is used by the natives as their live storage chamber for fish brought from the sea. It is covered with palm leaves.

the ship, one man standing in the stern of each to handle the long steering oar, his brown body, clad only in a lava-lava, glistening with coconut oil and his head and shoulders powdered with white dust.

With more shouting and laughter the baskets are caught up by the derricks, swung on board and dumped into the hold, sometimes missing and dropping their contents into the sea amid renewed merriment. If anything goes wrong with the derricks and the men in the surf-boats, rising and falling with the waves, are threatened with danger from above, they dive overboard to the safety of the sea, like frogs on the edge of a pond plunking into the water.

Sometimes the wind changes so suddenly that the ship is obliged to put out to sea in haste, and the surf-boats are caught before they are able to reach shelter in the small artificial boat harbor and are either swamped or driven upon the reef and thence hauled up on the beach.

THE RELATION BETWEEN THE NATIVES AND THE COCONUT TREES

Nauru is about seven and a half miles long and half as wide and is shaped like an oyster. It is bordered by the reef, which is bare at low tide, and inside of which is a beach of white coral sand. The beach above tide level is cov-

CATCHING RAIN-WATER FROM COCO-PALMS

Fresh water is scarce on the guano islands and must be provided by catchment areas for rain-water. When a coconut tree has a good bend in it, the natives wedge the butt end of a coconut leaf into the knee, which collects and diverts rain-water into a receptacle. Galvanized-iron tanks and concrete cisterns are also provided for storage.

ered with coconut palms, interspersed with pandanus and other trees and shrubs.

Back of the coconut plain rises a palisade of tall coral pinnacles whose summit is the phosphate plateau, which is covered by a forest of evergreen trees, the most common one being the tamanu (*Calophyllum inophyllum*), with handsome deep-green leaves, resembling laurel, and flowers like orange blossoms.

In the center of one end of the island is a small lagoon surrounded by a coconut grove.

The broad plateau is uninhabited, as the natives live only under the coconut trees.

The tie between the South Sea islander and the coconut tree has been dwelt upon by travelers; in fact, in the Nauruan legends the coconut itself either owes its eyes and mouth to human ancestry or man owes his eyes and mouth to the coconut—the legend is hazy in outline. Certain it is that it is the most precious gift of the gods to the dwellers on the coral isles, and where it does not grow, there are no inhabitants.

The green nut furnishes drink and a delicate meat like the white of a softboiled egg. The ripe nut furnishes the copra of commerce, food for man either raw or grated and mixed with other foods, as well as food for fowls and pigs and fish bait. It provides oil for the hair and skin, an essential part of the native's toilet. The dried and polished shells make water bottles and oil flasks.

The fiber which surrounds the nut in the husk is twisted into cord, sennit, used for every purpose where cord or rope is needed, from binding together the rafters and posts of huts, the timbers of canoes and palings of fences, to tying sharks' teeth upon spear blades and making bird cages and fish-nets.

The sap dripping from the severed flower stalk is sweet toddy, which fermented becomes soma toddy, an intoxicant. The unopened leaves in the crown of the tree make a delicate white salad, the "sailors' cabbage" of the old whaling days. As this can only be obtained by killing the tree, white people call it "millionaires' salad," owing to the valuation of trees.

The sheath at the base of the leaf (stipule) resembles a coarse sacking and is used for wrapping the grated meat in the crude oil press. The leaf makes an outside layer for the thatch, a coarse basket, broad coarse mats for the floor and for hanging on the weather side of huts. The midrib is used for fence palings and house walls. The dried leaves are bunched together and tied with green ones for torches. A strip of leaf bound around a tree trunk acts as a gutter for rain-water and a piece of leaf attached to the trunk in a certain way is a trespass notice.

The trunk of the tree is used for posts and rafters of huts, the shafts of spears, and dug-out canoes.

WEALTH IS MEASURED BY COCONUT TREES

Wealth and rank are gauged by coconut trees. To own much coconut land is wealth and aristocracy; to own none is beggary; in the old time it was slavery. Some men have made a good thing, as reckoned in the islands, by marrying brides rich in coconut land.

The land is cut up into very small plots, usually described by square rods and roods instead of acres. The title to the trees does not pass with the land, but is a separate transaction. You may buy a piece of land, but cannot use the nuts, and the native owner has the right to come upon your premises to gather toddy and nuts.

The present valuation of the trees is from one pound sterling each for bearing trees to one shilling each for properly planted young trees. The first British administrator on Nauru did not know this, and when he cleared a piece of government land for a cricket ground by cutting down 80 trees, the native owners asked and were paid 80 pounds.

The trees are not only reckoned by count, but the nuts are reckoned by count. In normal times the crop is continuous, blossoms, green and ripe fruit being on the tree at the same time.

In time of drought the natives are not permitted to make copra, as the nuts are needed for their own food and for seed.

From 1914 to 1917 there was a great drought which killed thousands of trees. When the rains came and the trees blossomed, the natives asked permission to make copra. The administrator ordered a census of the ripe coconuts, and he went in person all over the island and verified the count. The natives count quickly, by tens. Each heap contained so many hundreds. He found the total barely sufficient

THE ROAD OF HEART'S DESIRE

A road bordered with coral makes the twelve-mile circuit of the island of Nauru, following the beach for the entire distance. Only the tropics could afford the vision of beauty of a bright moon shining from a cloudless sky through the feathery fronds of the coco-palms.

to sustain the population until the new crop ripened, so forbade the making of copra.

THE PANDANUS TREE GROWS ON STILTS

The gods have given to the islanders another tree almost as valuable as the coconut and constantly associated with it. The screw pine, pandanus, is an extraordinary tree, dependent upon crutches and stilts. It starts in life as a stemless plant, closely resembling yucca, with sword-shaped leaves, each fitted on its edges and midrib with sharp spines. A little later it sends up a stout spiked trunk to about ten or fifteen feet, crowned with leaves like the radical leaves. It now resembles a huge mop.

Should the trunk be bent from the vertical, the tree drops from the top a cord with a bud at the end protected by a sheath; when it reaches the ground the sheath decays, the bud roots, and the stiffened cord becomes a crutch. A set of stout, bracing aërial roots is thrust out from the lower part of the trunk, the radical leaves decay and leave the tree standing upon stilts.

NATURE TRIUMPHANT AMID THE CORAL PINNACLES OF NAURU

A worked-out phosphate field is a dismal tract of land, with its thousands of upstanding white coral pinnacles from ten to thirty feet high. Yet, in this waste, vegetation begins and young pandanus trees and sprouting coconuts are here seen opening their vigorous leaves after having sent down strong shoots into the rock crevices.

A straight horizontal branch is often thrust out at a height of two or three feet from the ground, sustained by roots set at an angle on each side, resembling a rustic bench, but any attempt to use it as a bench is speedily abandoned, as it is set with stout spines. The tree grows thus with stilted roots till it covers a large tract of ground.

Pandanus leaves are used for making *ridis*, fine mats and basket weaving, for thatching huts, for calking canoes, and for many other things for which coconut leaves are too coarse. The tree bears an orange-colored globular fruit, the size of a foot-ball and larger, separable into sections, which are chewed for the flavor, as it is composed of fiber and flavor only. It is also stewed and the juice made into a palatable black paste.

SCRAP IRON USED FOR FERTILIZER

The coconut tree being of such supreme importance to him, one would think the native would cherish it as his wife and child, but, on the contrary, he gives it no attention whatever, for it grows without care and lives to a great age. If he wishes to plant a tree, he picks out of the heap a sprouted nut, whose flattened triangular husk and opening leaf, standing at right angles to the long petiole, resemble the body and head of a duck, sets it into a shallow hole in company with a piece of old iron, and leaves it uncovered.

The proper planting of trees is done in the same way, except that the holes are wide and deep and placed at regular distances. Iron rust is beneficial to young trees. The nuts are not covered with earth for a year.

In 1897 a scientific expedition from Sydney landed on the island of Funafuti, in the Ellice group, in order to put down a bore to ascertain the depth of coral. This was to test the theory of the formation of atolls as announced by Darwin, who had said that it could be settled by a core from a depth of 500 to 600 feet.

There had been a British expedition at Funafuti the previous year, which had been

THE NAURU ISLANDERS ARE DEVOTED TO THEIR PET TERNS

Known as "noddies," these birds of sooty body plumage and gray heads, classed with the "booby" because of their unusual stupidity, are pets of the islanders. Their eggs are collected for food.

abandoned on reaching a depth of 100 feet, owing to the breaking down of the machinery. The engineers had brought back a story of the difficulties in boring coral; that zones of extremely hard rock alternated with those of sand; that often the drill would strike a cave, where it would twine around in space and perhaps be lost in the depths.

It was with a good deal of trouble that money had been found for the second expedition. The government of New South Wales had furnished part, and private contributors the remainder, so that the little party felt that much depended upon their success. They began drilling and were only well started when a crown bevel-gear wheel broke and the boring stopped, as there was none to replace it. They stood around the drill in despair. There would be no ship calling for three months; there was no cable or wireless communication with the outside world; they were marooned on a tropic isle, whose discomforts and limitations they had discounted for science's sake, but which loomed in importance with the threatened failure of the expedition. A native stepped out of the crowd of curious islanders, whose bare bodies made a brown ring around the little group of white men, and, pointing to the broken wheel, addressed Professor David, the head of the party, in pidgin English:

"He no good?"

"No good!" was the reply, with a despondent shake of the head.

"One all saime belong me!" said the native.

"Belong you?" said Professor David in amazement. "What do you do with it?"

"Me plant him in coconut tree. You look see?"

The engineers did "look see," for the native dug up the twin of the broken wheel, which had been left behind with the discarded machinery of the previous expedition. It was put in place and the drilling went on. Mrs. David, who wrote what she calls "An Unscientific Account of a Scientific Expedition," has in her book a photograph of the "fertilizing wheel."

"A VEGETABLE GIRAFFE"

At first a coconut tree appears rather silly and inadequate. Mark Twain labeled it a feather duster on a long pole; Stevenson called it a vegetable giraffe, "so graceful, so ungainly."

We are so accustomed to think of a tree as having a solid vertical trunk, diminished regularly by branches, balanced and clothed with leaves, that a coconut palm hardly resembles a tree. It is bare to the top, tapering very slightly. I sometimes think of those sinuous trunks as ropes attached to captive balloons swaying in the wind. A fallen trunk ringed with the marks of decayed leaves looks like a great gray hawser; and yet this inadequate-appearing trunk suffices to sustain a tuft of leaves each ten and fifteen feet long and huge bunches of nuts eighty to one hundred feet in the air.

The coconut grove, seen from its edge, as one approaches from the sea, with its pale-gray slanting trunks and level tops, is without dignity and rather disappointing; but seen from within, the trunks become light, graceful pillars, the feather dusters become a roof of green, rustling thatch, the deep shade is a grateful shelter from the tropic sun; or, looked down upon from a hilltop, the massed crowns, moved by the trade wind, flash in the sun like drawn swords. From beneath and from above, the grove is stately and dignified and when the moon gleams are flashed from the great fans the heart swells with rapture.

It is a pleasure to penetrate the slender-pillared aisles, to hear the trade wind dashing the leaves high overhead, to follow the numerous narrow footpaths printed by bare brown feet.

The grove is not a solitude, but is the dwelling-place of the brown people of the island. Their huts stand all through the wood, but the gray thatch and mat-hung walls so melt into the boles of the palms that they are unobtrusive, and the people walk so lightly on their bare feet that they make no sound. It is startling to catch a slight movement in the shadows and see a group of men making a canoe; or to gaze into one of the brown pools of brackish water and see looking up the brown face of one of the maidens who is taking a bath; or to see on the edge of the grove a line of brown figures, with *ridis* swinging from hips, and bunches of drinking coconuts and a huge fish swinging on poles between them, silhouetted against the crimson sky.

The huts are furnished with nothing at all. Sometimes the floor or part of it is a platform, raised three or four feet; usually it is the ground, strewn with broken coral, covered with mats, on which the dwellers sit by day and sleep at night. There may be a Chinese camphor-wood chest, a clock, a lantern, a bicycle; there are always bottles of coconut oil and coconut-shell water-bottles hanging under the eaves.

The yard is walled by a line of coral a few inches high, like the play-houses we built when we were children, and it is often surfaced with clean white coral shingle from the beach.

Close to the hut are the graves of the household, sometimes inclosed by palings, but often merely outlined by coral or inverted beer bottles.

CIVILIZATION AND CLOTHES BROUGHT DISEASE

The cooking is done on the ground, outside the hut, and is very casual, for much of the food is eaten raw; raw fish, raw shellfish, and raw coconut are staples. When food is cooked it is generally burned outside and half raw within.

The native dress for both sexes is tasteful and becoming and suited to the climate. It is a full skirt made of narrow strips of pandanus reaching to the knees. A wreath of fresh flowers and a necklace of flowers or beads complete the costume. Sometimes the necklace is strung with shark's teeth and finished with a pair of frigate-bird feathers which hang down the back.

The men often wear a belt, in which is thrust a huge, wicked-looking coconut knife.

Although these people are almost nude, they do not appear naked; the brown pigment clothes them, and they are as unconscious and poised as we in our clothing. They have well set-up figures and walk with the ease and grace of persons who have never worn corsets or shoes. They have fine teeth and straight, black hair, that of the men cut short, while the women wear theirs streaming down the back or hanging in braids.

Owing to the influence of civilization, they sometimes substitute for the exquisite wreaths of natural flowers the pink celluloid combs sold by the trade stores, and the men wear extraordinary earrings, such as safety-pins and matches.

In the "good old days"—every country has its "good old days," and in the South Sea islands these were the days before civilization impinged upon native customs—the natives anointed themselves frequently with coconut oil. After coming in from the fishing canoes, after violent exercise, and always before sleeping they applied the oil freely. This safeguarded them from colds.

When they began to wear clothing they found that the oil stained their clothes, so they abandoned its use in great part.

All through the Pacific the native races are dying out, owing to their contact with the white races, whose diseases have proved extraordinarily fatal to them. So simple a disease as measles has almost destroyed the population of many islands. Tuberculosis is prevalent and Spanish influenza wrought great havoc.

Not the least cause of this is the wearing of clothing. The natives wear their clothes day and night. If they are wet by rain or by wading in the sea—I have seen them immersed to their shoulders while casting nets on the reef—they do not change, for in that climate they feel no sensation of cold, and even sleep in wet clothing, instead of oiling their bodies as formerly.

Many thoughtful observers hold that the influence of dress, especially the dress of women, has worked harm, for while the natives have learned to wear clothes, they have not learned how to wear them. Robert Louis Stevenson, who has much to say in praise of missionaries, says this about clothing:

"The mind of the female missionary tends to be continually busied about dress. She can be taught with extreme difficulty to think any costume decent but that to which she grew accustomed on Clapham Common, and to gratify this prejudice the native is put to useless expense, his mind is tainted with the morbidities of Europe, and his health is set in danger."

THE "MOTHER HUBBARD" IS ESPECIALLY UNSIGHTLY IN NAURU

The "Mother Hubbard" dress, the universal attire for women is worn in Nauru and reaches from throat to heels; in the Gilberts it is modified by being cut square in the neck and shortened to the knees. Fortunately, the missionaries stopped before they put hats and shoes on their converts.

A native woman does not feel herself modestly attired without the *ridi*; she often wears it under her dress, where you can see it bulge and hear it rustle. The missionaries devised a much more suitable dress for the men. The lava-lava, two yards of cotton cloth wound around the loins, tucked in at the waist and falling to or below the knees, and a white "singlet," a short-sleeved gauze undershirt, is simple and becoming. The *ridi* is frequently worn beneath the lava-lava for modesty's sake.

A large proportion of the Nauruans dress in purely native costume; others wear clothes to church or in the homes, where they are employed as servants, and change for *ridis* when they return to their homes; and yet others wear clothes without change till they fall into rags, or, as they say, "broken clothes."

The natives keep pigs, which run at large. "Captain Cook's pigs" they are called throughout the Pacific, as he is supposed to have introduced their progenitors.

One of the governors ordered all pigs penned. The owners built pens and put the pigs inside, but neglected to give them food and water, as they had never been in the habit of giving them any care, and they began to die; so the order was rescinded. The pork is delicious, as the pigs are fed exclusively on coconuts.

The natives also keep peculiar-looking chickens. The roosters have small bodies and abnormally long legs, so that they appear to walk upon stilts, while the hens are very small and lay small brown eggs. If this is a case of reversion to type, the rooster being descended from some long-legged ancestor and the hen from some tiny one, and if the tendency continues, there will come a time when the rooster will stand so high on his stilted legs and the hen will be so small and so far below him that they will not see each other at all.

The natives do not eat eggs, and the hens rear their broods unhindered, unless the owner desires to "catch shillings" in the white settlement, when he gathers all eggs that have not actually hatched and offers them for sale.

Tame frigate-birds are kept on large roosts close to the beach, and a favorite sport is catching the wild birds, using the tame ones as decoys; they are lassoed by a weight on the end of a fish-line. The children play a game in imitation of this, in which the bird is a pair of feathers weighted in the middle.

The birds which are not fully tamed are tied to the roost by long lines and are fed daily, just before sunset, with pieces of fish. The owner tosses the fish into the air and the birds swoop down and catch it. The native gives his pet water by squirting it out of his mouth, as the Chinese laundryman used to sprinkle clothes (see illustration, page 44).

FEW GODS IN THE ISLAND'S MYTHOLOGY

The native myths are not populous with gods, like those of richer lands. They say, in common with those of the other South Sea islands, that the sky originally lay flat upon the earth, and men wriggled beneath it prone upon their faces; when it lifted a little they went stooping; when it was finally hoisted to its place by the Spider, they stood upright. The first men were immortalized by being changed into coral pinnacles.

There appears to have been no organized priesthood, but an altar formerly stood before the hut of each chief, upon which were laid offerings of food, either devoted to gods, to the ghosts of their ancestors, or, what is more probable, to devils, in whom the natives have profound belief.

As late as 1889, a man-of-war called at the island and the sailors desecrated one of the altars by seizing the coconuts and other food upon it. The ship steamed away to Apia, in Samoa, was caught in the great cyclone on Saint Patrick's Day of that year, which destroyed most of the shipping in the harbor, including six warships, and was wrecked. The sacrilegious sailors were drowned. The Nauruans look upon this as a punishment by the spirits.

Some of these altars, which were coral pinnacles the height of a table and higher, are still standing, but are not used save as indications of the chiefs' houses. The government is substituting "chief posts" with the names of the chiefs inscribed.

The last of the witch doctors is still living, but the court has put an end to her practice. A native, whose abdomen was vastly distended by dropsy, sought her for relief. She took a woman's weapon, a short, stout handle with a head beaked with a shark's tooth, and ripped open the abdomen. The dropsy was cured, but the patient died, and the doctor was tried and convicted of murder and sentenced to life imprisonment in the house of the head chief, where she may be seen any day sitting on the mats in company with the chief's family.

AN ISLAND LYING IN LONELY SEAS

Nauru lies in lonely seas. There are three steamship routes between America and Australia, but the nearest one crosses the Equator about 1,400 miles to the east, on the way from Honolulu to Sydney; the steamship lanes across the Pacific from east to west lie about the same distance to the north; those from Sydney to Hong Kong about as far to the southwest. Once in three months a small steamer plying between Sydney, the Solomon Islands, and the Gilbert Group, trading in copra and carrying a few passengers, touches at the island.

The mission ship, *John Williams*, carrying missionaries of the London Missionary Society to and from their stations throughout the Pacific, calls once or twice a year. The Pacific Phosphate Company's cargo boats, which come up from Australia every three or four weeks, are the main connection with the out-side world. They carry mail, supplies, and a few passengers.

Time is not reckoned by the calendar, but by the arrival and departure of boats. The weather is never a topic of conversation, but the coming of the next boat is a vital subject.

TROPICAL HOUSEKEEPING

There are about 80 white residents. The greater number compose the "white staff" of the phosphate company—managers, clerical force, medical officers, engineers, overseers, and store-keepers. A garrison of a dozen men with a commissioned officer, a wireless staff, an occasional visiting missionary, the agent of the steamship company, whose boat calls four times a year, and the administrator, with his clerks, customs and post-office officials, make up the remainder.

Housekeeping has difficulties peculiar to the tropics. The houses of the white settlement are built of one thickness of boards and roofed with galvanized iron. The partitions stop about six inches below the ceiling, leaving spaces for ventilation. Wide verandas surround the houses, and these are the true living-rooms. The cook-houses are detached.

There are no wire screens. The almost constant trade winds keep away flies, but cockroaches as large as humming-birds fly in and out, and moths, lured by electric lights, dart against the ceilings. There are beautiful sphinx moths, which are caught by the natives, tethered by threads tied to their proboscides, and worn as ornaments upon their heads or shoulders.

Lizards, which scramble over the ceilings stalking flies, occasionally lose their footing and drop upon the head of any one beneath them. Rats make runways of the ventilating spaces; shore-crabs ravage gardens unless they are surrounded by crab-tight fences, and armies of ants attack cupboards and refrigerators unless they are defended by having their feet set in cups of water, which in turn must be covered with kerosene to prevent the breeding of mosquitoes.

All food is sent to the tropics in sealed tins, but as soon as they are opened weevils get in and work destruction. Every bed is fitted with a mosquito net, which must be cleared of mosquitoes that hide in its folds, before it is securely tucked under the edge of the mattress, if one would enjoy sleep.

THE SERVANT PROBLEM IN THE SOUTH SEAS

Wages are low; a native boy (all men employed as servants or in any capacity are called "boys") can be hired as cook for one pound a month; a house boy for fifteen shillings; a laundress, who brings one or two helpers and works two days a week, receives one pound a *month*.

The servants are fed where they work, but sleep in their own huts. These native servants are like any other, in that some are good and some bad. The good ones are treasures—faithful and honest.

The reader can see that residence in the tropics is not one grand, sweet song; that one does not merely open one's mouth to let fruits fall into it; but, notwithstanding these drawbacks, it has its agreeable side.

OCEANICA'S ISLES DE LUXE

The master of the moorings, a man who has spent thirty years in the islands is in the habit of saying, "The first ten years are the worst." Nauru and Ocean Island are really isles de luxe, for they have electricity for power and lighting; a refrigerating plant filled with beef and mutton supplied by live cattle and sheep brought up from Australia by each boat. Other advantages are a bakery, steam laundry, and plumbing with salt- and fresh-water shower-baths.

None of the other small islands has these luxuries; but, even without these, there is the charm of waving palms; of the shining beaches with their windrows of shingle, in which one gathers shells and coral; of the sea breaking on the reef; of the native huts glimpsed through the trees; of the white terns flying low and screaming; of tall herons wading in the shallow water at the edge of the sea; of the white clouds driven rapidly over the island by the trade winds; of the fleet of outrigger canoes sailing out at dawn or silhouetted against the setting sun as they return.

The climate is hot, but is tempered by the trade winds. For six months I watched the temperature range between 78 and 86 degrees; it rarely exceeds 90 degrees in any season. The sunshine in the middle of the day is blinding and scorching hot, but in the shade one suffers less than on many July and August days in the latitude of New York, in spite of the extreme humidity. About 4 o'clock in the afternoon the heat of the sun's rays becomes moderated and the evenings are delightfully cool.

SUNRISE AND SUNSET AT SIX THE YEAR ROUND

The sun rises at 6 and sets at 6 the year around; there is no daylight-saving there. The only change of seasons is when the "westerlies" come in the rainy season. These tropical rains descend with great violence. In the year following the three years' drought, previously mentioned, there was a rainfall of 150 inches, 10 inches falling in one night.

The violence of the wind resembles that of a blizzard, except that it is warm; but this is not a hurricane. The Line islands are not in the hurricane belts, which lie to the north and south of the Equator.

There is never any fog on these warm seas, and the brilliance of the moon and stars is unknown in the north. The pointers of the "Great Dipper," as it swings around in the heavens, are forever pointing to the Polar Star, forever out of sight below the horizon, and the "pointers" which mark the position of the Southern Cross are forever pointing at that rather feeble constellation, lying in the south.

The brilliance of the sunsets is beyond words; sometimes the whole sky is laced with streamers of crimson, changing to softest amethyst, with which the sea and the beach are tinted, while level bands of aquamarine stretch across the horizon behind the glowing streamers of color.

NATIVE CRAFT WITH ITS SAIL TIED UP TO "SPILL" A TOO-FRESH BREEZE

One of the characteristic devices of this boat is the outrigger, a piece of wood sharpened at both ends and fixed parallel to the length of the boat, which stabilizes the craft and even permits open-sea sailing without materially decreasing its speed.

AMERICAN WHALERS INTRODUCED A PIDGIN LANGUAGE

Nauru has its own language, which is not understood by other islanders. In common with all the Pacific tongues, it abounds in vowels, each of which is pronounced, so that a native talks with the mouth wide open.

In the intercourse between the American whalers and other white men in the Pacific and the natives, a quite workable language has been evolved, which is known as pidgin, *bêche de mer*, or beach la mar. Its foundation is probably Chinese pidgin, but it is full of words common to the islands. *Kai kai*, for instance, is the universal word for food; it is also the verb to *eat*; it is used humorously by white residents, who invite their friends to *kai kai*.

Belong, pronounced b'long, is in common use. A native does not say "My brother"; he says, "Brother belong me." You do not say, "What is your name?" You say, "What name belong you?" You do not send a servant to the store to *get* groceries; you send him to "*catch*" sugar, flour, etc.

A SAILING CANOE AND ITS CREW IN PRIMITIVE COSTUME ON JALUIT LAGOON:
MARSHALL ISLANDS

Jaluit, the chief island of the Marshalls, is an atoll with fifty islets on a reef. The lagoon around which these islets are grouped has a depth of 25 to 30 fathoms. Under Germany, Jaluit was the seat of government of the Marshall Islands and Nauru was assigned to that group, although the latter was 300 miles away and had its own language and distinctive customs (see text, page 24).

Bullamacow is the word for meat—either live cattle or canned meat of any kind. This is said to have arisen from the misunderstanding of their names by the natives when a bull and a cow were landed on one of the Samoan Islands.

COMMERCE CRAWLS APACE IN THE CAROLINE ISLANDS ADJACENT TO NAURU

The shed houses a fisherman's seine and the rickety stand holds the weight of his season's crop of copra, which he is trusting to the sun to get into a properly marketable condition for him.

SOCIAL LIFE AMONG
NON-NATIVE RESIDENTS

While society is small, it is an interesting little group of people, who are familiar with South Africa and India, who know the "Never, Never" of Australia and the mountains of New Zealand, and who always call the British Isles Home with a capital H. Their sons fell at Gallipoli and on the Marne, but they carry on.

Beer and skittles is a fact and not a mere saying. Skittles is played with nine pins, in a bowling-alley which had originally a long German name. Cricket is played, and tennis, and dinner parties are given with the formality of similar functions in civilized lands, save that the table is served by barefooted servants in lava-lavas, with wreaths of flowers on their heads, and there are dishes which are unknown to temperate climes.

Here one enjoys such food as the coconut-crab, or robber-crab, which climbs coconut palms for the fruit, lives in holes in the ground, and resembles a lobster in appearance and flavor; crayfish which are similar to those of the California coast; a great variety of fish, which are brilliant in color and delicious to the taste; the *pawpaw*, or mummy apple, a fruit which resembles a melon, but grows on a small tree; and sour sop, a variety of custard-apple which has a soft, white, subacid pulp, tasting like a fruit salad with *whipped cream*.

During the war there were many small functions for the Red Cross, as well as a play in the theater where the audience sits under the stars, and several fairs to which the natives contributed their shillings. In one of these there was a native market, managed by the chiefs, where pigs, chickens, and coconuts were sold for the cause.

> "There's a schooner in the offing
>   With her topsails shot with fire
> And my heart has gone aboard her
>   To the Islands of Desire."

What does it matter if the schooner is pervaded by the rancid odor of copra and populous with cockroaches, if natives traveling from one island to another share the deck space with the sheep and pigs? They are still Islands of Desire. The charms of the South Sea are real. Those who know them best love them most, and they gladly return from holidays spent at "Home" to take up island life with its limitations.

"A WIDE OCEAN, BUT A NARROW WORLD"

Would you like to do that, to cut loose from society, from convention, from civilization itself, and to sail and sail and sail, dropping familiar shores and landmarks; dropping the North Star, around which the whole familiar world revolves, around which history revolves—there is little history below the Line—and finally to make a landfall on a coral isle where coconut palms wave their shining fans above the dazzling beaches? It has been done many times; the palms are there, the natives are there, but they no longer look upon white men as gods descended by the rainbow bridge from the heavens; they have been disillusioned.

But let no one be deceived into believing that because these tiny islands are so remote, so lost in the sea, and society upon them so limited in numbers and so cut off from civilization, that one could flee to their lovely shores with the proceeds of crime, either stolen wealth or a stolen bride, and live an idle, luxurious life with the past safely concealed.

"The Pacific is a wide ocean, but a narrow world." Intercourse is not frequent, but it is constant; everybody knows everybody else, from Jaluit to Tonga, from Papeete to Port Moresby. Civil servants, missionaries, ship masters, traders keep up a system of communication that puts Marconi to shame, and just as in a small village gossip is more rife and uncharitable than in a large town, so it is in these small island communities.

YAP AND OTHER PACIFIC ISLANDS UNDER JAPANESE MANDATE

By Junius B. Wood

With Illustrations from Photographs Taken by the Author in the Spring of 1921

LIFE is easy and time drifts slowly by on the little tufts of green in the warm blue of the Pacific which now are under Japanese mandate. The largest is less than 13 miles in diameter, while a half dozen coconut trees, surrounded by nature's breakwater of mangroves, tells the whole story of many of the smallest. Nobody knows how many or how large they are. One careful estimate is 1,000 islands, with a total area of 970 square miles.

Sown in the form of an inverted T, the islands stretch 2,462 miles east and west, just north of the Equator, from Lord North Island, the westernmost of the Carolines, to Mille Atoll, the easternmost of the Marshalls; and 1,170 miles north and south from Pajaros, the most northern of the Marianas, to Greenwich, in the Carolines. Small as they are, they stake out about 1,500,000 square miles in the North Pacific.

Men of many nations—Portuguese, Spanish, English, American, French, Russian, German, and now Japanese—have wandered through the islands in the centuries since Columbus dared the unknown sea.

They came as explorers seeking El Dorados, soldiers to conquer new lands for their kings, pirates to recuperate in the balmy tropics, missionaries to teach and trade, "blackbirders" gathering laborers for the plantations of New Zealand and Australia, beach-combers drifting out their aimless existence, and all the strange medley of humanity that life's eddies cast into strange corners of the world.

Each has left a mark, a mere fleeting touch—the name of an island, a river, a mountain peak, or a family. But unconquerable nature is unchanged and the tropical jungle has covered the scars of their works, while the white skins darken with each generation of children and the family name is but a memory of an ancestor gone and forgotten.

They were but ripples on the surface. The old life runs along, deep and unchanged; the new is there for a generation, fading and disap-

A FEW OF THE TWO HUNDRED PERFORMERS IN PONAPE'S NATIVE DANCE

The men wear short fiber skirts, wreaths of flowers around their heads, and many strings of beads, while the women's costumes are as varied as a Fifth Avenue fashion show. The bodies of all the dancers, having been rubbed with coconut oil, glisten like polished bronze.

pearing in the next. At home amateur theatrical and movie companies don strange costumes to portray spectacles of departed ages. Here the past is masquerading as the present—whatever may be pleasing to the rulers of the day—and the costumes are as unique.

A GOVERNMENT IS POPULAR IN PROPORTION TO THE FREQUENCY OF HOLIDAYS

The last time our ship anchored in Ponape Harbor was on the Japanese national holi-

day celebrating the accession of the first mythological emperor. In 1921 it was the 2,581st anniversary.

During the hour's ride to shore in the little launch, winding between the sunken coral reefs showing white through the clear green water, the genial naval commander of the island explained that a holiday and big celebration had been arranged. Any government is popular with the natives in proportion to its holidays.

That afternoon the flag of the Rising Sun was flying over the big parade ground above the village and the naval band played the Japanese national air.

The natives were there to watch the athletic games, just as they or their fathers and mothers had come on other national holidays when the Spanish or German colors flapped in the breeze over the same parade ground and they joined in singing other patriotic songs in other languages. Some remembered the even earlier years, when Fourth of July was the big holiday, and a few could recall two occasions when bloody revolutions started against the Spanish rulers as part of the celebration of the American natal day.

Between the finish of a coconut-husking contest for native men and the start of a half-mile race for Japanese residents, in which merchants, officers, and sailors puffed and strained like real democrats, the busy little civil governor, tiring of the quiet monotony of a wicker chair under an awning, started to investigate the origin of a squat building between the Spanish church and the German school.

THE STORY OF A "BATH-HOUSE"

Of solid stone and mortar, with iron-barred windows and heavy doors, it had withstood time and revolutions. The governor said it was a bath-house. Several dutiful Japanese subjects corroborated his verdict and exhibited in mute proof one of the combination casks and furnaces in which they delight to parboil themselves after every day's work.

However, the Spaniards did not build block-houses of stone and iron for baths. The massive stone wall cutting off the end of the island where the settlement is located, just like the crumbling walls in Mexico and South America, showed their ambitions and fears ran in other directions

The wall in Ponape now is an ornament of the past. The Germans cut roads through it and vines cover its rough face.

"We'll ask this woman, her father was a German," said the governor.

A young woman sat under the shade of a tree, nursing a husky baby. A few weeks earlier she had been noticed at a native dance, her light skin contrasting with the other women, bare from the waist up, as they swayed and sung to the strange harmony.

The governor spoke to her in German. She shook her head, unsmiling and uncommunicative. The language of her father was already forgotten. The question was repeated in choppy Nipponese to a young Japanese, who translated it into the native vernacular.

"She says the Germans used it as a chicken-house," he explained.

"And what was it before it was a chicken-house?" asked the governor, like a real antiquarian.

Nobody in that ladies' nursing circle knew. Why worry about the past or future when there is nothing to worry about in the present, is Ponape philosophy.

THE GERMANS MADE THE NEW GUINEA NATIVES POLICEMEN

By this time Governor Okuyama had his dander up. Something must be found out. Leaning against a tree was a study in black and white, an outsider among the straight-haired, brown-skinned natives. Shirt and trousers were white; feet, hands, and face were inky black, with a jaunty white cap on his woolly pompadour.

"He's from New Guinea," the governor explained. "The Germans used them as policemen, because they are so black the natives are afraid of them."

The former local terror, though he understood both German and English, could not remember farther than the chicken-coop era; but, true to his police training, he went to find out. He returned with a report that it had been built and used as a jail. He added that several of its inmates, hurried to an untimely end, were buried under its cement floor, promising disturbed dreams for those who doze in its modern bathtub.

INQUIRING FOR A BOY IN AMERICA

The foot-race was finished and the governor flitted to distribute the prizes to the winners. An old man approached timidly. A smile encouraged him.

"You American?" he asked in his little used English.

It had been ten years since the last American missionary had left the island. Possibly there is some similarity among Americans.

"A Ponape boy lives in United States," he said.

"Whereabouts in United States?" I asked.

He shook his head hopelessly.

"Just United States," he replied. "Perhaps you know him," he added, for in all of Ponape's continent—of 134 square miles—everybody knows everybody else, as well as some of the great men on the other islands, to them far away.

"Perhaps. What's his name?" I suggested, knowing a few hundred out of America's 110,000,000.

"Uriel Hadley. He's a Ponape boy," he repeated, a touch of pride in his quiet voice.

There was no Uriel among my memory of many Hadleys, and his face fell in disappointment. He could not understand that anybody could live in America and not know the "boy from Ponape." Something was wrong, but he did not know why.

I walked away from the noisy games through one of the gaps the Germans had made in the thick stone wall, past the silent church, and along a path rapidly growing narrower, as it passed from the little fields which the Japanese were cultivating into the ever-crowding jungle.

I stopped to look across the jungle-closed valley to where the late sun was tinting the palms on the mountain top, just as it had done in the dim, forgotten days when Ijokelekel came in his war canoe. The pit-a-pat of bare feet approached along the path. It was the old man, one of the coconuts salvaged from the husking bee in his hand.

"Are you a Ponape boy?" I asked as he stopped.

"I'm Ngatik boy; can't go home," he said, uncovering another of the tragic romances of the Carolines.

AN AMERICAN SAILOR'S COLONY ON NGATIK

He pattered along down the path, carrying his day's harvest, his exile and the story of Ngatik forgotten. In the early, '60's an American whaler was wrecked on Ngatik, 75 miles southwest of Ponape. Visioning a choice assortment of heads to hang from the eaves of their huts, the natives attacked the survivors.

But the sailormen were well armed, with the result that most of the ambitious warriors were killed, and the new arrivals settled down to a life of laziness and a plethora of wives until the next wandering whaler sighted the lonesome island and took them home. That accounted for the old man's familiarity with English.

"You like coconut?" he asked with native hospitality, proffering his entire meal.

"I live here, men's hotel," he explained, as the gift was declined. He trotted off on a side path through an opening in the bush.

In a little cleared space stood the "men's hotel." It was a roof of thatch, open on all sides. Fastened to the poles supporting the roof, about four feet from the ground, was a braided hammock-like floor of fibers and leaves. Cracking the coconut on the fringe of rocks which protected the hotel from the crowding jungle, he climbed to the unsteady floor, squatted on his haunches, and started the evening feast, his day's work done.

Down at the foot of the path where the narrow bay separates the main island from the rocky head of Chokach (one of 33 islets surrounding Ponape), half a dozen outriggers were tied to the mangroves. Other bare feet were coming along. An athletic young man, a wreath of flowers on his head and a shirt of fiber strings covering his hips, untied one of the canoes. The little narrow hull, hollowed from a single tree trunk, was so narrow that his knees rubbed as he sat on the cross-bar.

"Want go Chokach?" he offered.

"I'm Pingelap man," he vouchsafed, as his narrow paddle drove the canoe across the quiet water.

Hospitable, good-natured, and easygoing, the Ponape natives have a temper which flames into wild revolt when pressed too hard. The first Fourth of July revolution against the Spaniards, in which the governor and four others were killed, a carpenter being the only one able to escape to the warship *Maria Molina*, was precipitated when a road boss forced the natives to pick up rubbish with their hands.

The next revolution, in 1891, started over the rivalry between an American mission church and a new one established by the Spaniards near Metalanim Harbor, on the east side of the island. The natives disposed of an officer and twenty-five soldiers who interfered in the religious competition, and when a larger force of two officers and fifty soldiers was sent from the garrison at Ponape their worldly worries ended with similar celerity.

A transport with 3,000 soldiers came from the Philippines. It went ashore on the reef outside of Metalanim, and in the ensuing mêlée, according to the widow of the American adventurer who later piloted the transport off the reef, three natives and 1,000 soldiers went to another world to settle their religious differences.

That ended the local holy war until 1898, when the five tribes on the island were having a lively fight among themselves, which Spain, on account of its trouble with the United States, was too busy to meddle with.

After that Germany exercised the lien which it had held on the Carolines and Marianas since 1886 and bought them from Spain.

About noon, on October 18, 1910, the young German overseer of a gang of natives building roads, or rather footpaths, on Chokach struck one of the men with a whip. That was not the first occasion, but it was the last.

Governor Gustav Boeder, of Strassburg, a retired army officer, who heard of the riot and death of the overseer, hurried from his headquarters on the hill overlooking the settlement. He believed that his presence would awe and quiet the natives. He was paddled across the same narrow bay which I was crossing. As he stepped ashore, a bullet fired from the hillside struck him dead. The rifles captured in the Spanish days had been brought from the hiding places.

HEADSTONES TELL TRAGIC STORY

Four granite headstones, on which are neatly chiseled their names, ages, and the

THE GRAND FINALE OF PONAPE'S MUSICAL COMEDY AND GRAND SOIRÉE
(SEE TEXT, PAGE 71)

The four girls and eight men in the center of the lawn, the stars of the performance, are going through the evolutions of a wand drill and an expurgated "hula," for which the "chorus" forms the customary background.

date—October 18, 1910—in the little foreign cemetery, tell the story of that day.

A month or so later a German warship happened to anchor in the harbor. The natives were as peaceful as ever, but there were no officials. "Joe of the Hills"—Joseph Creighton, a London gipsy, who lived with the natives, away from the settlement, and died in Ponape only last year—was the only foreigner alive to tell the story.

The force from the ship rounded up the inhabitants of Chokach. Half a dozen ringleaders were shot, others were imprisoned, and the remainder—about 200 men, women, and children—were deported to the barren phosphate island of Angaur, in the West Carolines. To repopulate Chokach, other natives were brought from Ngatik, Pingelap, Mokil, and Mortlock islands.

"Mrs. Anna lives Chokach," said the boatman as he lifted his canoe into a canoe-house, a thatch roof under which were a dozen outriggers, either on the ground or on cross-beams tied to the roof-poles.

Who "Mrs. Anna" was I did not know, but the affable young native said she spoke English and German, and we started along the well-built path which encircles the island. Evidently she was a local personage of importance.

ON THE KITI RIVER, PONAPE: CAROLINE ISLANDS

Back of Ronkiti, the port of Ponape, there are practically uninhabited tracts of level country crossed by many streams with cascades suitable for conversion into water-power for industrial use and of sufficient volume to float rafts and large boats.

THE WOMEN CARRY THEIR TOWN FROCKS AROUND THEIR NECKS

Stretches of the path hugged the shore and hillside. In other places the water would be hidden by the dense foliage.

The little houses were scattered on each side, none of them more than a hundred yards away. A few were of rough boards, one had a corrugated tin roof, but most of them were thatch roofs, woven palm-leaf walls, and roughly smoothed floors, worn shiny by many bare feet and slumbering backs. All were elevated on posts. When the weather is wet, it is very wet.

The rockiest spots also were selected for building sites. Let nature fight the battle with the jungle.

A NATIVE MANSION IN THE CAROLINE ISLANDS

The dwellings, which are usually surrounded by a neatly swept clearing devoid of grass, are built upon platforms to keep the floor—the family bed—as dry as possible, for the ground is at times deluged with tropical rains.

A little boy with no more clothes than when he was born and a girl with a few feet of calico for a skirt were driving a family of goats. Occasionally we met a barefoot man or woman. Some of the men wore trousers and under-shirts; most of them had only the knee-length, artistic fiber skirt hiding their loin-cloth.

The women, like their sisters in lands where dress is more of a problem, had a town gown and a home costume which meant no dress at all, merely a cotton skirt reaching below the knees. Most of them walking toward the village carried the town wrapper comfort-ably looped around their necks, ready to be slipped over their shoulders when the settle-ment was reached.

MEETING THE WIDOW OF A FAMOUS SCIENTIST

"Mrs. Anna now," said the man. A tall, straight old lady was slowly approaching. She stopped at the sight of a stranger. Her thin gray hair was smoothly parted in the middle. Many years of of tropical suns had not browned her to the colors of the other natives. Tattoo-marks on the backs of her hands ran across the wrists and disappeared in the loose sleeves of the immaculately clean wrapper. Other designs showed on feet and ankles.

"I'm Mrs. Kubary," she said. This, then, was the relict of that striking character on whose studies much of the scientific knowledge and romantic lore of the Carolines is based, who came to Ponape when a youth of 19, full of enthusiasm and vigor, won a name for himself which reached to Europe, and wrested a wealth of coconut groves from the jungle, only to be conquered in the end, when age weakened strength and courage.

The day the fight relaxes, the jungle, always waiting, starts to reclaim its own. A monument in the little cemetery, with a bronze slab sent by his scientific colleagues in Europe, showing the profile of a strong face, with drooping moustache and eye-glasses, and the legend, "Johann Stanislaus Kubary, 1846-1896," epitomizes his hopeless life story.

The jungle has choked the botanical garden which Kubary started and closed the paths across the mountains which the warrior trod in the days when Ponape had a population of 60,000 instead 3,000. Some say that the rifles captured from the Spaniards are hidden in that jungle.

A new path around the edge of the island, built under Japanese supervision, past the houses of its remaining fringe of population, is the only route of communication by land. Lieutenant Yamanaka, the present naval commander, treats the natives with gentleness and consideration.

Seated on a rough rock at the side of the Chokach footpath, the woman, who is said to have been received at court in Berlin, and in Hamburg society in the early '90's, when she was a tropical belle, patiently told her story. Then she was 25 and handsome; now she was 56 and faded. The tropics had reclaimed her, quick and sure.

"My name is not Kubary now," she added, as if following the thought. That was another miniature of the changing life of the Carolines. When the struggle seemed never to be won, Kubary committed suicide.

The widow, still a young woman, married a young native. He was one of the leaders who killed the German governor and was executed. The widow and her daughter—she has flown from the jungle—were among the 200 deported to Angaur. The older has returned to take another young native husband. The young man in that little world who has the Kubary widow for a wife has social standing if not domestic contentment.

HER FATHER WAS A BALTIMOREAN

"My father was Alec Yeliot, of Baltimore," she continued. "He was buried here by Dr. Doane (one of the early American missionaries). I was 14 years old when I married Mr. Kubary. We traveled through all the islands while he made his studies for the Godefroy Company, and then we went to Europe.

"We went everywhere—England, France, Germany, Italy, Russia—but so much has happened to me since and nobody here understands it that I have forgotten. Only a year after we were back Mr. Kubary died, leaving me and our daughter. She is now a teacher in the French convent (naming a British city). All of the past is gone, but life goes on just the same.

"My father came from over the seas and my husband from another land. Our girl has gone, for she was of their race, but I have come back. The islands never change, and these are my people and my life."

THE LARGEST AND MOST PRETENTIOUS CHURCH IN PONAPE: CAROLINE ISLANDS

This edifice, originally built by Americans, was remodeled by the Spaniards, and services are now conducted in it by native leaders.

She folded her tattooed hands over her knees, showing thin through the cotton wrapper, and silently gazed across the bay to where the Japanese transport was riding at anchor. For a few hours each month that reminder of the outside world breaks the monotony of Ponape; otherwise life flows along smoothly and contentedly, unthinking of the past or of tomorrow.

TATTOOING ADORNS THE BELLES OF OLDEN DAYS

Formerly the natives were walking pictorial histories. After the missionaries came, tattooing was discouraged, not caring to be tattooed themselves, and in recent years it has been prohibited. It was considered a sign of courage, without which a young man or young woman was not worthy to marry. This practice even went so far as systematic mutilation of the sexual organs. Scientists are divided whether this, an epidemic of smallpox brought by a whaler, or the frequent tribal wars are responsible for the diminished population.

The young people still practice an effete modification of the old tests of courage by pricking cicatrices, or little raised welts, on their flesh. Most of the girls prefer the right shoulder for the adornment, though some have

AN ALTAR OR TOMB IN THE SUN TEMPLE OF NANMATAL,
PONAPE: CAROLINE ISLANDS

Beneath this altar there was once a large room with an underground passageway leading outside the walls of the mysterious city (see text, page 66).

them on their breasts. The boys adorn shoulders and chests.

The welts, which are formed by making a fairly deep cut in the flesh and keeping it open until the new skin grows into a ridge, are usually about an inch long and a quarter of an inch wide. Sometimes they are arranged in straight lines, one for each admirer, like the bangles on a high-school girl's friendship bracelet; again they may make an asterisk or are scattered indiscriminately over shoulders, breast, and back.

The older people still show the old adornment, the lobes of the ears stretched into loops until they touch the shoulders, and bodies and limbs tattooed, the most distinctive effect being broad parallel stripes of solid black from ankles to thighs. However, they follow modern conveniences and wear the long loops wrapped around the ears close to the head when they work, while skirts drape the gaily tattooed legs of the social leaders of former days.

That night there were open-air movies and Japanese sword dancing by sailors and a couple of proficient native boys on the lawn of the official residence. Visitors and dignitaries had chairs, while the others stood or squatted on the cool grass.

Movies were a novelty to the natives but comparatively few had the energy to walk the quarter mile from the settlement to the grounds. An American comic of an indestructible man wrecking furniture, and pictures of Japanese warships, including a boat crew feverishly lowering a cutter, were the hits of the evening.

PORTION OF THE WALL SURROUNDING THE ANCIENT CITY OP NANMATAL,
PONAPE: CAROLINE ISLANDS

Numerous narrow, straight canals, now overgrown with jungle, encircle the walls. (See reference in "The Islands of the Pacific," page 16, and text, pages 66 to 73.)

THE MYSTERIOUS CITY OF NANMATAL

Late that night, when the others were sipping the inevitable tea on the broad veranda, I slipped away down the long hill toward the settlement. In a pocket was a little map in India ink and water colors which Kubary had made in 1874 of the ruins of Nanmatal, the city of stone walls and canals off the east coast of Ponape which has outlived the facts of its origin (see illustrations on pages 65 and 68)

Storms through countless generations have filled the broad, straight canals until the sands are dry at low tide, but the walls of heavy basaltic monoliths, in some places 30 feet high, have withstood typhoons and earthquakes, proof of a civilization forgotten when Quiros came, in 1595, and found the natives living then in flimsy houses of thatch and sticks.

Charles Darwin, F. W. Christian, the Rev. MacMillan Brown, Dr. Amberg, and others of greater or lesser fame have delved in the ruins near Metalanim harbor and evolved theories of their origin. They do not agree whether the patch of land, 1,200 yards long and half as wide, once was a tropical Venice or whether through the ages it has been gradually sinking, swallowed by sea and smothered by vegetation. The waves still beat against its massive seawall, while hundreds of little shell rings, used for money and necklaces, can be found even today.

One incident chronicled by all the scientists, like the fragment of bone from which the archeologist reconstructs a dinosaur, is that a metal spear-head was once found in the ruins; and another, less generally known, comes from Capt. John J. Mahlmann, of Yokohama, that, 40 years ago, he copied two Chinese ideographs carved on one of the big stones. However, the whereabouts of the spearhead is unknown and the letter, which the English captain sent to Shanghai, was lost, and he never could locate the stone again.

Some say modern buccaneers built the city of stone without the natives knowing it; others trace it to the copper age, and the present Japanese claim it was the work of their ancestors, who built the uncemented fort in Osaka.

A similar deserted city stands in the hills on the mainland of Ponape, back of the port of Ronkiti, on the southwest corner of the island. Near this is the home of Henry Nanpei, a remarkable native chief, who has traveled extensively in Europe and America and is the bulwark of the Christian work on the island. He probably could tell more about the ruins than any other man; but the scientists have confined their researches to Nanmatal, which is more easily accessible.

Kubary first searched Nanmatal for Godefroy's museum, and when Governor Berg was in the islands he shipped so many specimens to the Leipzig Museum that the government sent an expedition to clear away the jungle and study the city and the slightly different ruins on the island of Kusaie.

The latter adjoin the settlement, and as soon as the expedition left, the natives directed by an unawed American planter, supplemented the visitors' labors by using a good portion of the uncovered walls for building a breakwater and pier, greatly to the wrath of the Leipzig students of ancient history when they heard about it, a year later.

After his last visit to the Nanmatal ruins, Governor Berg died suddenly, justifying the native superstition that the gods punish intruders.

The present governor has a big white book in which visitors, either after exploring Nanmatal or discussing it in the cool of his residence, are requested to write their opinion of its origin.

The sight of the massive walls, silent and impressive, still surrounded by the narrow, straight canals and overgrown with jungle, is worth the blistered back, wet feet, and skinned shins necessary to reach the ruins. However, as each student has a different verdict, the present method, more reassuring for governors, and less strenuous for visitors, may be equally conclusive.

NIGHT ON PONAPE

The broad road from the headquarters residence to the village below was a silvered path between black walls of trees. Only the stars were in the sky that night, and nowhere are they as bright as in the tropics.

Through the still air from a native settlement along the bay came the occasional thump of a drum and the echoes of laughter. The big parade ground was silent and deserted, the old Spanish wall and the new Japanese schoolhouse ghostly in the starlight. No spooning couples were in the village park.

A YOUNGSTER OF PONAPE STANDING ON THE THRESHOLD OF THE ISLAND'S
MOST ANCIENT TEMPLE

Nanmatal, off the east coast of Ponape, was a prosperous city of stone walls and canals hundreds of years ago.
Its origin is lost in the folklore of the islanders (see text, pages 66 to 73).

The local police turn in early in Ponape. The governor says he has arrested only twenty-two men, all for stealing. One took a bottle of sake from the Japanese store and the others eloped to short distances with their friends wives.

As the authorities discourage primitive methods of vengeance, local home-wreckers are put in jail.

The house where I was going was dark, but alive with the deep breathing of many sleepers. It was a pretentious dwelling, long and low, like

THE FINEST TYPE OF
NATIVE MISSIONARY

Though the American missionaries abandoned their
work on the island of Truk years ago, the Reverend
Ham Aettu still preaches the gospel to his people.

a field barracks, with a narrow porch along the side, on which opened the rooms for different families. A "Hello!" brought an answering shout, and I stepped through an open door into darkness. Somebody appeared with a lantern.

My host and his family had been sleeping according to the custom of the tropics. The wife slipped on a skirt, and he with two stretches was fully clothed in shirt and trousers. He took the lantern and we went into the residential social hall, a room with a table and two chairs and a waist-high wall on three sides. The men and boys, who had been sleeping on the floor, pulled their mats outside and continued to snore.

KUBARY'S MAP OF NANMATAL

The map which Kubary had made nearly half a century ago, with its water colors showing land and water, and each ruined building drawn to scale, was spread on the rough table under the smoking lantern. Each site had been numbered, corresponding to a list of names in native dialect down the side, like a city visitor's guide, showing the theaters, railroad stations, and leading hotel.

"Those are our names for the city," he said.

There were thirty-three which Kubary had identified and nearly as many more about each one of which this man told some story. One was the king's castle; others were the prince's castle, temples, forts, sepulchers, and holy places which common people must not enter.

Nanmatal means "in many openings," and the other native names were translated on the map into such crude descriptions as "great castle," "on the corner," "in the largest breakers," "coconut castle," "shadow of a tree," "under the chasm," "in the sepulcher," and so on for half a hundred buildings.

THE MERCHANT MARINE AND NAVY OF MOEN ISLAND ON REVIEW IN
TRUNK LAGOON: CAROLINE ISLANDS

About forty of the little islands of Truk are scattered about in this big lagoon, which could accommodate our largest transatlantic liners.

"My grandfather was an American, but it is hard to translate the names," he said. "My father was a native, but I have an American name. I want to go to America some time."

He pointed out the burial temple, where Governor Berg did his last excavating; the broad inclosed stretch of water, now filled with sand, which had been the inner harbor, and the wide entrance used for an anchorage when storms did not lash the sea-wall. His spirit seemed to go back to the past glories of that distant age.

"Here's where the canoe stopped," he mused, putting a finger on an unmarked spot on the south side of the ancient city.

"What canoe?" I asked.

"That's only a story," he said. "We're Christians now and don't believe those stories any more. It's only what the old natives tell."

NATIVE STORY OF THE MYSTERIOUS CITY

However, from his refusal to accompany me to the ruins and the reluctance of any natives to visit them, their superstitious belief in the dangers of the present world seem to outweigh their confidence in the safety of the future. He told the story, and it is probably as good a version of the rise and fall of the mysterious city as any which the scientists have concocted.

"Once two brothers, Oleosiba and Oleosoba, came to Ponape. They became chiefs and joined all the tribes in Ponape into one tribe. They wanted a great city and just asked for it, such was their power, and it came down from the sky just where it is at Nanmatal today. The other city, at Ronkiti, was built in the same way, and one brother lived in each city, ruling over the island. After them for hundreds of years there was only one king in Ponape. Soutolour was the last.

"When he was king, Ijokelekel, a warrior from Kusaie Island, which we call Kodou, came to attack the city. He had only one canoe and it carried 333 men. They reached Ponape in the night, and when day broke they saw the thousands of palms on the mountains and thought they were warriors, and were afraid to attack and went back to Kusaie.

PONAPE BETRAYED BY A WOMAN

"Ijokelekel came again in his canoe with 333 men and circled the island. Each day, from a distance, they saw the palms and were afraid to come closer, but went home a second time. When he came a third time he went only half way around the island and put the canoe into the harbor at Ronkiti. He sent some of his men ashore. Their instructions were:

" 'If you see any people ashore and there is an old woman among them, run back to the canoe, for I will go ashore and stay with her tonight.'

"Soon the men came running back, saying they had seen an old woman. Ijokelekel went ashore and found her. That night, as they talked, he said:

" 'There are many warriors in Ponape.'

"The old woman replied that there were few men, but many women on the islands, and that the warriors from Kusaie should stay and make their homes there.

" 'But I have seen your warriors standing by the thousands on the mountain tops,' said Ijokelekel.

"Then the old woman, proud to show her knowledge, as all women are, laughed at him and answered:

" 'They are only palms, and what you think are the waving spears of the war dance are only their branches blowing in the breeze.'

"Ijokelekel had learned what he wanted. He ran back to the canoe and they paddled around to Nanmatal. At daylight they attacked the city. Here is where they left the canoe.

"Jauteleur, a great warrior, led the men of Ponape. They fought for two days, and each night the warriors from Kusaie were beaten back to their canoe.

CORRECT "STREET" CLOTHES IN TRUK

This one-piece poncho-like garment is the prevailing style in the Caroline Archipelago. When the wearer is working or away from the settlement, he throws it aside, leaving his waist and shoulders bare. Both the men and women of the older generation are tattooed, but this practice is now prohibited.

"On the third day Jauteleur was again pushing back the strangers when one of the warriors from Kusaie drove a spear through his own foot, fastening it to the ground. The other warriors, who were running away, saw that their comrade stayed to fight, and came back to help him. They captured the city."

NANPARATAK, THE PONAPE ACHILLES

My host stopped, lost in reverie, dreaming the romance of those stirring days. Civilization, with its laws and conventionalities of distant lands, has substituted work and worry for that care-free life. This man, a native leader, was interpreter for the Japanese chief of police. He might have been an Ijokelekel or a Jauteleur in another age.

"I have forgotten the name of the soldier who won the fight," he said, lapsing again into silence.

The name wouldn't come. He called in the rough Ponape dialect. The light step of bare feet came along the narrow porch. Leaning over the low wall was a woman, bare from the waist up, straight-featured, with threads of gray in the smooth black: hair, sharp-eyed and strong muscled, as if a bronze Venus of fabled Nanmatal had been conjured into the dim light of the flickering lantern. Without raising his head, the man spoke in their native language.

"Nanparatak," she said. Homer would have picked a better name for the South Seas Achilles. I wrote it down while the jargon was fresh. When I looked again the dusky vision had disappeared as silently as the mythological Helen of Troy. The legend of Greece and that of Ponape have strange points of similarity.

"Jauteleur and Soutolour were killed, and Ijokelekel divided Ponape into five tribes, just

THE BEST HOTEL IN TRUK: CAROLINE ISLANDS

The guests sleep on especially prepared platforms, and an individual may surround his particular corner with nets or leaves for privacy and protection from mosquitoes. There is always plenty of fresh air, as the house is open on all sides.

as they are today," he resumed. "But they did not live in either of the cities, for the gods who had built them were angry. Nobody has lived in them since, and when people go to them it rains and thunders, for the gods do not want them to be disturbed. Nobody has disturbed them since the German governor died."

A DANCE ON PONAPE, CENTER OF THE JAPANESE MANDATORY ISLANDS

On another day the natives gave a dance. It was a good show, but, considering the elaborate preparations and number participating, sadly abridged and expurgated. Saddened by

THE CHEFS OF TRUK PREPARING FOR A COMMUNAL FEAST

The breadfruit has been scraped and quartered and the shoots of the banana are being spread on the red-hot stones in preparation for the baking.

the march of events in America, somebody wrote, "You Cannot Shimmy on Tea," and probably the same applies to the South Seas. The League of Nations very wisely specifies prohibition for all the natives in its mandated possessions, but a reasonable ration on dancing days would undoubtedly put more "pep" into the performances. Nobody became overheated on this afternoon. At that, it was the best dance seen on any of the islands.

Ponape is about the center of the Japanese mandatory islands. Its life and customs may be taken as a standard for all the others. Those who have passed their lives along this border of the Equator say it is the cleanest, healthiest, and happiest. Conditions and habits vary in the others; some are better and some are worse, according to the individual tastes.

Each group of islands has a language of its own. The years are not long past when each

FISHERWOMEN HAUL THE SEINE IN TRUK: CAROLINE ISLANDS

They advance in a long line, holding the big nets in each hand, and thus form a wall as they drive the fish into shallow water. Daily practice has taught them the proper moment to wheel into a circle and land their catch.

A GROUP OF NATIVE MEN OF WOLA, A SETTLEMENT ON THE ISLAND OF TRUK

The natives pierce the lobes of their ears and load them with such heavy weights that they expand to enormous proportions. The hill tribes of Truk are darker in color than the people of the coast, who are of light reddish-brown hue.

"ALL MEN'S HOUSE," OR BACHELORS' CLUB, IN TRUK: CAROLINE ISLANDS

The club is the common sleeping place for any man without a home, as well as the storage shed for disabled canoes and other rubbish. It usually has a roof of thatch and is open on all sides.

was a petty kingdom, and the stranger cast up on its shores was hailed as a gift from the gods, whose head quickly adorned the door post of the first islander to greet him.

The extent of American missionary activity can be gauged by the length of the women's skirts. In Yap, which missionary influence has hardly touched, the fluffy fiber upholstering clings precariously on the hips. In the Marianas and middle Carolines, skirts start above the waist-line. In Kusaie, the easternmost of the Carolines, they reach to the shoulders in one-piece wrappers. In the Marshalls, where the missionary work has flourished without interruption, the long trained wrappers, sweeping up the dust are further ornamented with high ruffle collars and wrist-length sleeves.

YAP VISITED BY A SERIES OF DISASTERS

The native of Yap is little concerned over the controversy which is waging in other parts of the world as to who shall rule his rocky home. Just now, his chief worry is to get enough to eat. War and the elements have

PENGAL VILLAGE, PORT LOTTIN, KUSAIE: CAROLINE ISLANDS

Kusaie well deserves its soubriquet of "Garden of Micronesia." On Lele, an islet of Kusaie, it is said that there grows a species of wood admirably suited to shipbuilding, being tall, perfectly straight, and of great durability.

completed the blight which has cursed the islands for a decade. When the English cruiser sailed past and shelled the wireless station out of existence, and a few weeks later a Japanese transport arrived and deported the foreigners, including the solitary policeman, the islander's chief source of income was gone.

The final blow came on December 7, 1920, when a typhoon leveled the vegetation on the islands, destroying most of the coconut palms, breadfruit trees and other food supplies.

The last previous typhoon had been on February 20, 1895.

About the time the new coconut trees were ready to bear, one of those strange plant sicknesses of the tropics spread over the island. The new groves, which had been patiently planted, were just coming into fruit when the last typhoon wiped out everything.

To everybody in the world except the islander himself, the location of Yap is of importance. It is about 250 miles east of Palao,

THE FRONT YARD OF THE TOMIL CLUB-HOUSE: YAP

The ground around the building is covered with flat stones, and here many of the native conferences and dances are held. The man in the picture is leaning against one of the yellowish limestone discs that were formerly used as money on the island (see text, page 81).

the future Japanese naval headquarters of the mandate, which is some 500 miles east of the Philippines, about opposite Mindanao.

YAP ISLANDERS WERE LEADERS

Like the other forty-eight so-called islands in the Carolines, Yap is not a single island, but a cluster of small islands. There are ten islands in the group, four of which are fairly large and volcanic, all surrounded by a coral reef about 15 miles long and 4½ miles across at its widest point. Epp, the native name for Yap, is the largest of the four. North of it, and separated by narrow straits, are Torei, Map, and Rumong. Tomil is the name of the harbor and settlement, with a good anchorage, reached by a narrow passage and past dangerous rocks.

In native civilization, the islanders of Yap were the leaders and teachers for all the others. Most of the legends and customs of the old

A TYPICAL NATIVE HOUSE AT KORROR: PALAO ISLANDS

Inside the stone platform in front of the dwelling the family dead are buried. Each household has its own cemetery.

THE CLUB-HOUSE AT KORROR, SEAT OF GOVERNMENT OF THE PALAO ISLANDS

This house was at one time a village, but the German governor had it moved opposite his office. where it stands today. Its remarkable appearance, both the inside and outside being extensively carved, has remained unaltered.

ONE OF THE UBIQUITOUS CLUB-HOUSES OF THE CAROLINES, NEAR TOMIL: YAP

This is where the traveler, if he be a man, meets the men of the islands to discuss politics, crops, and the high cost of living, and to hear stories of the daring deeds of bold chiefs, love intrigues, and the gossip of the Pacific.

days can be traced back to Yap. Some islands improved on their lessons, others never advanced beyond crude imitations.

Stories are told of men from Yap coming in their canoes as far as the Marshalls, more than 2,000 miles away. They taught the others navigation. In the Marshalls, where the little low-lying patches of sand and coral are close together, they improved on the knowledge of the men of Yap until the seamanship of the old Marshall chiefs, sailing unerringly without

compasses, reading the waves by day and the stars by night to lay their course, is a puzzle to modern navigators.

The story of the two brothers. the genesis of the legendary history of Ponape, is told with variations of names and incidents to suit the local dialects and events in the Marshalls and other islands. The brothers are supposed to have come from Yap. The Yap natives built houses, towering structures for that part of the world. In Palao, to the westward, they im-

A MEETING OF THE "BIG CHIEFS" OF THE PALAO ISLANDS ON KORROR

He of the helmet is the Aybathul, a chief of first rank and practically king of the Palaos. He and one other member of the group are wearing bracelets of bone, symbols of dignity. The handbag of plaited leaves carried by each chief is the Palao equivalent of a cigarette case or tobacco-pouch, for it contains the "makings" for betel-nut chewing.

proved on the architecture of Yap, while as one travels eastward to the Marshalls the structures become of decreasing simplicity.

The natives of Yap knew how to make earthen bowls and cooking utensils, how to weave baskets and ornaments, and how to dye the fibers various colors. They had houses where only the chiefs met, club-houses where the unmarried men lived and which all the villagers could enter on certain occasions, and canoe-houses for the use of all. The same custom prevailed on the other islands.

In Yap the women cultivated the taro beds, and on the other islands they did the fishing. All agreed that the women should do the work and the men the fighting and loafing. With the advent of ships and trading, the men now work and the war canoes are leaking and decaying.

AN ISLAND OF STONE MONEY

Yap had a currency of its own—big circles of yellowish limestone which nobody could steal and smaller pieces of pearl shell with squared edges. They were brought from Palao, which gave them an intrinsic value. However, just as they discarded the fire-stick when matches were obtainable, the crude money is no longer used, except as ornaments or to sell to curio-collectors.

THE COUNCIL-HOUSE OF KORROR CHIEFS: PALAO ISLANDS

The building, which is placed on a structure of stones about four feet above ground level, is ornamented inside and out with pictorial carvings painted white, red, black, and yellow. The ordinary villagers, and especially the women and girls, are strictly forbidden to darken its doors.

The big money resembled a flat gristmill wheel with a hole in the center, so two men could carry it on a pole. Pieces four feet in diameter are numerous, and I was told that one wealthy and exclusive club had an 11-foot coin, but I could not find it. About two feet is the usual size. A three-foot coin could purchase a young pig; so the fortune-hunter could take his choice of paddling to Palao to quarry a piece of loose change and risk drowning while returning home, or of carefully raising a shoat.

The money, leaning against the elevated stone platforms of the clubs or homes of leading citizens, is practical as well as ornamental. The number and size of the piece mark the building's financial standing, and when visitors come they sit on the stone pavement, resting their backs against the stone cart-wheels, as they leisurely discuss club politics or the latest escapades of the village slave girls. The smaller shell money is now used for necklaces.

Some of the club-houses in Yap are more than 100 feet long and 30 feet wide, built on platforms of rough stone paving. The roofs are striking—high and narrow, with the gable longer than the eaves, so that it projects several feet on each end. A similar type of architecture is followed in the more pretentious homes.

Posts and beams of the club-houses are carved and painted, usually in red, black, and white, with scenes of historical events on the island. In Palao, the club-houses are even more elaborate, the favorite ornamentation being a rude figure of a profusely tattooed woman straddling the door, as a warning to the village maidens to be circumspect. The natives' houses also are partitioned in a way, at variance with the usual one-room publicity.

THE WOMEN WEAR SMALL "HAYSTACKS"

The natives have built good roads in Yap, in most places well paved with stones. The women do all the work around the homes, but the men are sturdy workers and more efficient than those on any other of the islands.

Though they are anchored rather low, the skirts of the Yap women are longer than those of any other wearers of the garments of palm fiber and hibiscus bark. They reach to the ankles and are so full and fluffy that they look like small haystacks. The more fancy ones are dyed variegated colors.

A SHRINE ON KORROR: PALAO ISLANDS

This structure, three feet wide and six feet high, is a miniature replica of the club-house shown on the opposite page. Though it is a place of worship, it contains no idol or image.

In Palao the women wear a double short skirt. The men of Yap wear a short shirt of the inner bark of the hibiscus over their loin-cloth, while those in Palao usually dispense with it. In a part of the world where the mother's hip serves as a baby carriage, the full skirt of Yap makes a convenient seat for the youngster. Even the smallest girls wear skirts.

Possibly the most important part of a Yap woman's apparel is a neck-string of thin native cord. This she puts on as soon as she is of mar-riageable age. Nothing else is worn above the waist, and it is considered brazenly immodest for a woman to appear without the cord around her neck. A long, thin comb of wood, which the men wear in their hair, shows similar distinc-tion. A man's rank or standing in the communi-ty is indicated by the length of his comb. Some measure 18 inches.

Many learned pages have been written on whether the Yap natives, with their ingenuous ways, sufficient for their simple needs, or the Marshall islanders, With a semblance of West-ern customs imposed on their old habits and tropical atmosphere, are the more civilized. They are extremes geographically as well as extremes between the old and the new. The missionaries say that the Marshall islanders are both civilized and Christians.

TWENTY YEARS WITHOUT A MURDER IN THE MARSHALL ISLANDS

The Marshalls are proud of their record of twenty years without a murder and very few cases of theft. That is more than any American city of equal population and farther removed from days when head-hunting was popular can boast. The missionaries have taught the natives that they must not smoke, dance, play cards, cook on Sundays, drink liquor, or indulge in various other relaxations which are not consid-ered an eternal bar to godliness in other lands. Calisthenics were abolished in the mission schools because the movements suggested the dances of their forefathers to the young people. As all these restrictions economize physical effort, the natives willingly accept them.

On the other hand, the population is said to have diminished 5o per cent in as many years, and the medical officers at the free hospi-tal say that 90 per cent of their patients have

"LET THE WOMEN DO THE WORK," IS THE SLOGAN IN ROTA: MARIANA ISLANDS

The little girls keep the street around the school-house clean by sweeping it during the recess period, while the boys go out to play.

venereal diseases and 60 per cent are also suffering with *frambesia tropica*, otherwise known as "yaws," which might be avoided if the rudiments of hygienic cleanliness were observed.

THE ANCIENT DANCE IS NO MORE

Though there is little to disturb their lassitude, the Marshall islanders are happy and contented. Most of them sit around their houses all day, have a song service in the evening, and then go to sleep.

Walk past a native house almost any hour of the day and two or three men or women can be seen lying on their backs in the cool interior.

They will lazily roll their heads to look through the windows, opening on a level with the ground, to see who is passing, but more than mere curiosity is needed to dislodge them from their braided mats. It has been so long since there has been anything much to do that they have gotten out of the habit.

They do not have the vigor of their forefathers, when the men, working themselves into a frenzy in the war dance, dashed to their canoes to battle with the people of a neighboring island. Those were the days when the women danced the wild *rü-ong*, whose sinuous gyrations were the sensation of the South Seas. Four years of training, until her backbone was

TRAVELING A LA MODE IN SAIPAN: MARIANA ISLANDS

Taking an afternoon drive on some of the South Sea Islands combines all the leisurely and luxuriant features of an airing for some people in some portions of the United States.

as flexible as a snake's, were required before a girl was permitted to join in this dance. In those days, to avoid argument, children traced their name and ancestry to their mother.

The chiefs and most of the men who have been educated in the mission schools have added a familiarity with foreigners and business methods to their native shrewdness. Many of

them speak English, and, with their innate love of politics, deluge the visitor with questions on the outside world and international affairs, some of which are too complex for the ordinary traveler.

The years of missionary teaching in the islands have made the natives a peaceful, friendly, and hospitable people, and their even

STUDENTS OF READIN', 'RITIN, AND 'RITHMETIC IN ROTA: MARIANA ISLANDS
The slate is the private property of the pupil, while the text-books belong to the school.

THE SCHOOL AT JALUIT CONDUCTED BY THE JAPANESE AUTHORITIES
The pupils are obliged to remain for at least three years of instruction. Jaluit is the chief island and administrative center of the Marshall group.

MAIN STREET IN A VILLAGE OF ROTA: MARIANA ISLANDS

All the houses are elevated above the ground and have small windows under the overhanging thatch roofs, some of which extend out beyond the house to form a sort of porch. The woman in the foreground has spread mats on the sidewalk and is drying cocoa beans.

longer association with American and later Australian, German, and Japanese traders has given them a knowledge of values. It has been many years since a pink comb could be traded for a cask of coconut oil in the Marshalls.

"Yak we yuk" is the invariable greeting from man or woman. The salutation, "Love to you," may be taken to symbolize their daily spirit. They have seen much of Americans— rough sailors with pirate instincts, fighting and robbing; others who married their daughters and settled in the islands, and, finally, the gentle missionaries, who built schools and churches. America has taught them much, and they dream of America, far across the Pacific, as their adopted country.

"WHAT IS HAPPENING IN AMERICA?"

Possibly it is a chief, or a native preacher, or a man or woman who has studied in one of the mission schools, who always calls when an American visits one of the islands. A present of a gaily bordered mat, an assortment of artistically woven fans, a fish-hook made from shells or some other native handicraft is always brought. And when the visitor leaves the baskets of fresh coconuts which are sent aboard his ship will quench his thirst for many days.

As clothes have become popular, tattooing has disappeared. Once a chief was tattooed from ears to waist, in fine lines of many designs, entirely different from the broad stripes of the Carolines. "Chief Moses" is the only survivor of that age and though he now wears a high collar, his cheeks are lined as if they had been branded with an electric toaster.

Lebario, with nine atolls under his control, is another of the old chiefs, a grim, serious-minded man, whose life has registered all the changes in the Marshalls. My first sight of him was at Wotje. He was busily dictating a contract to his stenographer, a fat, middle-aged man with an ancient but effective typewriter. The captain of the Australian trading schooner was waiting to sign it, and Lebario was in a hurry, as

FISHING IN DEEP WATER IN A WRAPPER AND A LARGE CONICAL HAT
MUST HAVE ITS COMPLICATIONS

Since being introduced to this passé garment of civilization, the native women make peculiar use of it. They can scarcely be persuaded to dispense with it when they go fishing. In some of the islands they keep it strictly as a town gown, which they don on the road when they get in sight of the houses of the settlement (see text, page 61).

the bi-monthly ship sailed for Jaluit in a few hours and he must catch it. However, he had time to stop all work and ask the invariable question, "What is happening in America?"

EVENINGS AT THE "CLUB" IN THE MARSHALL GROUP

Dramatic stories are told of the early days, only half a century ago, before the Marshall islanders became pupils of the Western World. Then these low-lying islands—more than 300,

grouped into 32 circular atolls, with a total land area of only 156 square miles—were a world of their own, each atoll having its chief and usually at war with all its neighbors.

More than one night, when the moonlight was silvering the beach and the rest of the settlers slept, we sat until morning in the cabin of Joachim De Brum while old men reminisced of their boyhood.

Legends which their fathers handed down to them, love romances of island Cleopatras, and daring deeds of bold chiefs, stories of the

GIRLS OF THE CHAMORRO TRIBE
IN SAIPAN: MARIANA ISLANDS

The Chamorros are not of the same stock as the natives of the Carolines, but are probably allied with some of the Philippine tribes. They dress in European style and show a preference for white clothes. They also wear leather sandals, a style not common to any other South Sea islanders under Japanese control.

rough characters who had come in later days, whispered locations of still buried treasures of tortoise-shell and gold, arguments of crops and prices of today—all were mixed in an incongruous medley. And, much like clubdom the world over, a sleepy boy would appear with an armful of coconuts the "eyes" deftly extracted, for story-tellers and audiences always are thirsty.

De Brum is a remarkable character. Born on the islands, son of a Portuguese trader and native mother, subscriber to an American daily newspaper and several magazines, he keeps in touch with the greater world thousands of miles away though the mail steamer never comes oftener than once in two months.

VALUABLE COPRA CROP PRODUCED BY THE MARSHALL ISLANDS

Life in the Marshalls today is denatured and commercialized. The transformation came quickly, once it started. Though they were discovered by de Saavedra in 1529 and explored by Captain Marshall in 1788, it was not until 1886 that Germany took possession of them as a colony.

In a part of the world where men's wealth is measured by coconut trees, the Marshalls are a valuable asset to any country. They produce more than half the copra from the Japanese mandatory. Each island is a waving crown of palms. Periodically the fierce typhoons strike this or that atoll, leveling the trees, decimating the inhabitants, or even lifting an entire island from its shallow bed on the coral reef, but the total producing power of the group is hardly affected. In five or six years new trees have grown, and those of the inhabitants who temporarily migrated in search of food and shelter return to their home island.

While the Marshalls are entirely low coral islands, the Carolines are both volcanic and coral and the Marianas are entirely basaltic, five of the Marianas—fifteen in number when Guam is included— having active volcanoes. One diligent statistician has located 680 islands in the Carolines, divided into forty-eight clusters. These latter are what show on maps as individual islands.

PLETHORA OF NAMES
FOR EACH ISLAND

Truk or Ruk, meaning "mountain" in the native language, where the Japanese naval headquarters administering the mandatory is located for the present, is the largest of the clusters. It consists of eleven volcanic islands, one of which is four miles across, and some 80 coral islands, most of them extremely small, all surrounded by a roughly circular reef 35 miles in diameter. About half the little islands are on this reef, and the remainder are scattered in the big lagoon, which can be navigated by the largest ships.

The Japanese have followed the practice of the men of other nations, who ruled for a day or a year over the islands, and have given Truk a new crop of names. Nearly every island in the Carolines has a Portuguese, Spanish, Russian, French, English, American, or German name in addition to its assortment of native titles. Mariners' charts, compiled mostly from data of the American missionary schooner *Morning Star* or English surveys, are fairly impartial to all nations, but many other names are used by sojourners in the islands.

Though they show as yet only on official communications, the Japanese have renamed the eleven larger islands in Truk after the seven days of the week and the four seasons, those on the reef after signs in astrology and palmistry, and the small ones inside after flowers.

The three groups in prehistoric ages may have formed parts of two mountain ranges of which the peaks still are above the waves in the Carolines and Marianas, while only the encircling reef of the tireless coral remains in the Marshalls.

The natives of the Marianas differ physically from the natives in the Carolines and Marshalls. Many show traces of European blood and their language includes expressions from the Tagalog and Spanish of the Philippines, possibly traced to the days when Spain ruled the islands. Many of their homes in Saipan are large and comfortable, in European style, with pianos and other furniture which is not found farther south.

The Kanakas, as the natives of the Carolines and Marshalls are called, who also are in Saipan, retain their native customs—absence of clothes, chiefs' houses, and dances to the full moon.

Tribal wars, with victories measured in the number of warriors' heads and women captured, mixed the blood on the islands long before the white men came, and since that time migration has been easy and safe, until racial characteristics are blended and indistinct.

IN THE SAVAGE SOUTH SEAS

BY BEATRICE GRIMSHAW

Miss Grimshaw is an enterprising young English woman who recently passed several years in Fiji and the New Hebrides on a search for good opportunities for investment. She explored many unknown sections of these islands and has written a delightful narrative of her travels and experience, "Fiji and Its Possibilities." The following article is abstracted from this book, and is printed here through the courtesy of the publishers, Messrs Doubleday, Page & Company of New York.

FIJI is a British colony, situated in the southwest Pacific, lying between the 15th and 22nd parallels of south latitude and between 157 east and 177 west longitude. It consists of 155 islands, with a total area of 7,400 square miles. Most of the land is contained in the two great islands of Viti Levu (Great Fiji) and Vanua Levu (Great Land), which account for 4,112 and 2,432 square miles respectively. These two islands are exceptionally well wooded and watered, and could, it is said, support three times the population of the whole group. Viti Levu is in every way the most important island in the archipelago. It contains the seat of government, the principal harbors, all the roads, and much the greater part of the colony's trade. There is one town in the group besides Suva—Levuka, the capital of former days, on the small island of Ovalau.

The climate is certainly hot, though the thermometer does not rise to any extraordinary heights. During the three hottest months—January, February, and March—the highest shade temperature ranges between 90° and 94° Fahr., and the lowest between 67° and 72°, roughly speaking. In the cooler months of June, July, and August, 59° and 89° are the usual extremes. The air is moist, as a rule, and in Suva, at all events, one may safely say that a day without any rain is almost unknown. On the northern side of Viti Levu the climate is a good deal drier and in consequence less relaxing. Dysentery is fairly common, but there is no fever to speak of, and the climate, on the whole, is considered healthful. Mosquitoes are so troublesome that most of the better class of private houses have at least one mosquito-proof room, with doors and windows protected by wire gauze.

A ROOT OF YANGGONA FROM WHICH THE INTOXICATING DRINK OF THE FIJIAN
ISLANDERS IS MADE

DRYING VANILLA, FIJI

VANILLA PLANT AND BEAN

As we pass down the main street of the capital, the curious mixture of the population is very noticeable—whites, half-castes, Samoans, Indians, Chinese, and, more conspicuous than any, the Fijians themselves—tall, magnificently built people of a color between coffee and bronze, with stiff, brush-like hair, trained into a high "pompadour," clean shirts and smart short cotton kilts, and a general aspect of well-groomed neatness. They do not look at all like "savages" and, again, they have not the keen, intellectual expression of the Indians or the easy amiability of the Samoan type of countenance. They are partly Melanesian, partly Polynesian in type, and they form, it is quite

evident, the connecting link between Eastern and Western Pacific.

East of Fiji, life is one long, lotus-eating dream, stirred only by occasional parties of pleasure, feasting, love-making, dancing and a very little gardening work. Music is the soul of the people, beauty of face and movement is more the rule than the exception, and friendliness to strangers is carried almost to excess. Westward of the Fijis lie the dark, wicked, cannibal groups of the Solomons, Banks, and New Hebrides, where life is more like a nightmare than a dream; murder stalks openly in broad daylight, and music and dancing are little practiced and in the rudest possible state.

In Fiji itself the nameless, dreamy charm of the eastern islands is not; but the gloom, the fevers, the people of the west are absent also. Life is rather a serious matter for the Fijian, on the whole; he is kept in order by his chiefs and by the British government, and has to get through enough work in a year to pay his taxes; also, if the supply of volunteers runs short, he is liable to be forcibly recruited for the armed native constabulary, and this is a fate that oppresses him a good deal—until he has accustomed himself to the discipline of the force, when he generally makes an excellent soldier. But, all in all, he has a pleasant time, in a pleasant, productive climate, and is a very pleasant person himself, hospitable in the highest degree, honest, good-natured, and clever with his hands.

A MARVELLOUS TRANSFORMATION

The whole penal apparatus is one gigantic jest, and is regarded as such by most of the whites and not a few of the natives.

To begin with, there is hardly any real crime, what there is being furnished chiefly by the Indian laborers employed on the estates of

A FIJIAN IN FESTIVAL DRESS

A FIJIAN IN SUNDAY DRESS, FIJI

the Colonial Sugar Refining Company. The Fijians themselves, though less than two generations removed from the wild and wicked days of the Thakombau reign, are an extremely peaceable and good-natured people. In the fifties and sixties, and even later, murder, torture, and cannibalism were the chief diversions of a Fijian's life, and the power of working one's self into a more violent and unrestrained fit of rage than any one else of one's acquaintance was an elegant and much-sought-after accomplishment. This change, effected largely by the work of the missionaries, but also by the civilizing influences of the British government and of planters and traders innumerable, is most notable. Nothing can be more amiable and good-natured than the Fijian of today.

Yanggona (the "kava" of the eastern Pacific) is the universal drink of Fiji. It is the hard, woody root of a handsome bush (the *Piper methysticum*) which grows freely in the mountains. The Fijians prepare the root by grating or pounding, pour water over the pounded mass, and strain it through a wisp of bark fiber. The resulting drink looks like muddy water and tastes much the same, with a flavor of pepper and salt added. One soon gets to like it, however, and drunk in moderation it is extremely refreshing and thirst-quenching. The Fijians do not drink moderately, I regret to say; they often sit up all night over their yanggona, drinking until they are stupefied and sleepy and quite unable to walk, for yanggona taken in excess paralyses the legs for

MALEKULA WARRIOR, NEW HEBRIDES

an hour or two, even though the head may be quite clear. The British government has forbidden the ancient method of preparing the root, in which it was chewed and spat out into the bowl, instead of being pounded. For all that, yanggona is very frequently chewed at the present day, when no white people are about.

There are no woods in the world more beautiful and valuable than the woods of Fiji, although want of capital and, to some extent, want of enterprise has prevented their becoming widely known. "Bua-bua," the boxwood of the Pacific, is very common and grows to an immense size. It weighs 80 pounds to the cubic foot, is very hard, and most durable. The "cevua," or bastard sandalwood, a strong-scented, very durable wood, grows freely in logs one foot and two feet in diameter; and the real sandalwood is also found, though not plentifully. Another useful wood is "vesi," which grows two and three feet in diameter. It is much like teak— hard, heavy, and extremely lasting in the ground or out of doors; it is also rich-colored and very easily polished. The "dakua" is one of the most valuable woods; it much resembles the New Zealand kauri pine and grows to a large size, sometimes six and seven feet in diameter. It contains a great deal of gum, and quantities of this can be taken out of the ground wherever a tree has been. The timber is useful for almost any purpose. The "yaka" might be called the rosewood of the Pacific, if it did not also, in some degree, resemble mahogany. It is a wood of the greatest beauty, being exquisitely marked and veined and taking a high polish. This is a wood that certainly should be known to cabinet-makers, and no doubt will be later on. The "savairabunidamu," a curious dark-red wood, is extraordinarily tough, and can be steamed and bent to almost any shape—a valuable quality. The "bau vundi" is a kind of cedar, very workable and most lasting. A singularly beautiful timber is the "bau ndina," which is deep rose-red in color, tough and firm, and suitable for engravers' use. Besides these, there are more than sixty varieties of other woods, all useful or beautiful and most to be found in great profusion. The quantities available are very large.

THE WOMEN'S DANCE

DANCING AND SINGING SCENES IN NEW HEBRIDES

BRINGING OUT THE MUMMY FROM THE "HAMAL" (SEE PAGE 101)

TYPICAL IDOLS IN A NEW HEBRIDES VILLAGE (SEE PAGE 102)

UNCANNY INSECTS

The wonderful stick insects of Fiji, familiar in all home museums, are found in nearly every cocoanut tree. They are very ill-smelling, and squirt a fetid fluid at one's eyes, if handled. Leaf insects I never saw, except when the natives caught and brought them to me, but all the guava bushes have them, although a white man's eye can seldom distinguish them from their shelter. They are most miraculous and uncanny creatures, absolutely leaves endowed with the power of motion, so far as the most scrutinizing eye can see, for even their legs and heads are a precise copy of stalks and small leaflets.

A certain enterprising man and his wife, who were getting rich very slowly indeed keeping a country store, resolved to try whether the magic bean might not do for them what it had done for others in South America and the West Indies. So, in the face of some actual opposition and continual ridicule, they expended their little capital of 250 pounds on the leasing of eight acres of warm sheltered valley land and the planting of 9,000 cuttings of good Mexican vanilla.

For three years, with the assistance of one Fijian and occasionally a couple of Indians, the industrious couple kept their plants weeded

LOOKING OUT FOR TROUBLE   THE ALLIES COMING IN

Villages are surrounded by stockades made of interwoven reeds

and tended, and latterly looked to the fertilizing of the flowers—a rather tedious business, done every day by hand, in the earliest hours of the morning; and at the end of the three years the reward came, for the plants were yielding splendidly and were expected to give about 9,000 pounds of dried beans, bringing an average price of 10 shillings a pound. The fruits of the first season were just coming in when I visited the plantation, and the lucky young couple were counting up their gains, present and future, with joyful hearts.

SULLEN NEW HEBRIDES

The New Hebrides are not very far from Australia—only about 1,500 miles northeast of Sydney—and they are by no means an insignificant group, since they extend over seven hundred miles of sea, and some of the islands are sixty and seventy miles long.

The native population is variously estimated at 60,000 to 100,000, and there are about three hundred French settlers and less than two hundred British and colonials, most of whom are missionaries.

POISONED ARROWS

The islands are extremely beautiful and remarkably fertile. Three crops of maize a year can be raised with little trouble. Coffee is largely grown, and there is none better in the Pacific. Millet, for broom-making, grows readily and pays well. Copra can be produced in the New Hebrides to better advantage than in any of the British Pacific colonies, the Solomons only excepted. Eighty nuts a tree is considered a very good average over the greater part of the South Seas. In the New Hebrides the figures I received seemed almost beyond belief, but, even allowing for much exaggeration, it seems certain that the average yearly crop of nuts must be quite twice

as large as in Fiji, the Cook Islands, or Tonga. I saw more than one tree that had three hundred nuts at once upon it (as I was informed; I did not count them, since that would have involved going up the tree with a paint-pot and a brush to mark them off), and I heard of one or two that had four and even five hundred.

This is a more important matter than might appear at first, for the copra trade is the true gold-mine of the Pacific. The oil that is expressed from the dried nut kernels is used in many different departments of commerce, especially in soap-making, and the demand constantly exceeds the available supply—so much so that the well-known firm of Lever Brothers have been buying up large tracts of land in the British Solomons to keep their factories supplied.

The popular idea of the New Hebridean, for a wonder, comes very near the truth. He is supposed to be, and is, treacherous, murderous, and vindictive. Yet there are a few things to say in his favor. He is wonderfully honest—so much so that in the bush districts a coin or a lump of tobacco found by the wayside will never be appropriated by the finder, but will be placed in a cleft stick at the edge of the track, for the real owner to take the next time he may chance to pass that way; and if the possessor never returns, the "find" will remain where it has been placed until some white man or some "civilized" native from a plantation passes by and appropriates it.

One of the strange things seen in one village was the collections of boars' tusks belonging to the chiefs. These were displayed on a long stand that exactly resembled eight or ten bazaar stalls joined together. There were some hundreds of them placed in long rows—how many exactly I had not time to count, as I heard that the canoes were just coming home from the mainland and I wanted to be on the shore to meet them. Many of the tusks were curved into a complete double circle. These are greatly prized, but are only obtained at the cost of much suffering to the unlucky pig that furnishes them. He is tied up in a house and never allowed to wander forth, for fear of destroying his tusks. From each side of the jaw the teeth that oppose the tusk and prevent its going too far are removed, so that in time it grows right round through the unlucky animal's flesh and provides a splendid double armlet for the native who owns the pig.

In Malekula, one of the larger islands of the New Hebrides, many a married woman was distinguished by a dark gap in the ivory-white teeth of her upper jaw, where the two middle incisors had been knocked out with a stone. This extremely unpleasant substitute for the wedding ring is found in various parts of Malekula. The operation is performed by the old women of the tribe, who greatly enjoy the revenge they are thus enabled to take on the younger generation for the injury once inflicted by their elders upon them.

By a good deal of worrying and a little tobacco, I persuaded the villagers to show me a mummy from one of their "hamals," or sacred houses.

It appeared to be the stuffed skin of a man fastened on poles that ran through the legs and out at the shoulders. The fingers of the hands dangled loose like empty gloves. The hair was still on the head, and the face was represented by a rather cleverly modeled mask made of vegetable fiber, glued together with bread-fruit juice. In the eye-sockets the artist had placed neat little circular coils of cocoanut leaf, and imitation bracelets were painted on the arms. The face and a good part of the body were colored bright red. The ends of the stretcher-poles

were carved into a curious likeness of turtle heads. Standing up there in the dancing light and shade of the trees against the high brown wall of the hamal, the creature looked extraordinarily weird and goblin-like. It had a phantom grin on its face, and its loose skinny fingers moved in the current of the strong tradewind—it certainly looked more than half alive.

MAKING A CONICAL HEAD

It was while I was staying with the kindly and hospitable B——s that I had the chance of photographing what I believe has never been photographed before—the making of a conical head.

A good many years ago certain men of science who had procured skulls from all parts of the world were struck with the extraordinary egg-like shape of some that came from Malekula. No one knew much about the people who owned these remarkable heads, and science forthwith erected rather a pretty theory on the basis furnished by the skulls, placing the owners on the lowest rung of the human ladder and inferring that they were nearer to the ape than any other type at that time known.

Later on some one happened to discover how it was that the skulls came to show this peculiar shape, and the marvel vanished when it was known that compression in infancy was the cause. It is still, however, a thing curious enough. Several other nations compress their infants' heads, but none seems to attain quite such a striking result as the Malekulan, in those districts where the custom is systematically practiced. A conical head, when really well done, rises up to a most extraordinary point, and at the same time retreats from the forehead in such a manner that one is amazed to know the owner of this remarkable profile preserves his or her proper senses, such as they are. I could not hear, however, that the custom was supposed to affect the intellect in any way.

"It would be hard to affect what they haven't got," a trader observed on this subject.

The conical shape is produced by winding strong sinnet cord spirally about the heads of young babies, and tightening the coils from time to time. A piece of plaited mat is first put on the head, and the cord is coiled over this, so as to give it a good purchase. The crown of the head is left to develop in the upward and backward fashion that is so much admired. One fears the poor babies suffer very much from the process. The child I saw was fretful and crying and looked as if it were constantly in pain; but the mother, forgetting for the moment her fear of the strange white woman, showed it to me quite proudly, pointing out the cords with a smile.

She had a normally shaped head herself, and it seemed that she had suffered by her parents' neglect of this important matter, for she was married to a man who was of no particular account. A young girl who was standing beside her when I took the photograph had evidently had a more careful mother, for her head was almost sugar-loaf-shaped. It is interesting to know that this well-brought-up young woman had married a chief.

STRANGE WOODEN IMAGES OF ANCESTORS

A visitor to the island of Malekula, New Hebrides, is greatly impressed by the huge images in the amils, or village squares; they are rudely carved, barbarously painted, and are called "temes," or images of the dead.

These images differ greatly from each other. Some are made of wood, others of the butt of a fern tree; some are painted in scrolls or stripes, others in rings; some display only a head, others are rude effigies of the whole human body; in some the eyes are round, in others oval-shaped.

The colors employed in olden times were coral lime, yellow ocher, a mineral green, and charcoal. Civilization, through the trader, has supplanted the green and yellow with the laundry blue and red lead. They are more brilliant, no doubt, but less in keeping with their surroundings.

A remarkable fact is, that although the images are rude in design and out of all proportion, they are real attempts at portraying the human figure. Every part is carefully put in; yet, with the exception of the boar's tusks on one, there is an entire absence of the combination of the human and animal, as, e. g., in the Hindu pantheon. This is possibly due to imperfect and rudimentary notions of divinity, if these are at all gods. There are no figures, like the Ephesian Diana, denoting the nourishment of man and beast from many-breasted Nature. There are no many-headed or many-eyed emblems of the omnipotence or omniscience of the gods. We are still among the lowest and rudest forms of religion.

The people of Tanna, another island of New Hebrides, are a remarkable race and, in spite of their murderous tendencies, have a great deal more character than the Malekulans. Queenlanders know them well, for thousands of Tannese have been employed in the Queensland sugar country from time to time. Whatever they may have gathered of civilization in Australia stays with them but a little while after they leave. On landing they generally take off all their clothes, go back to their villages, paint their faces, and take a hand in the latest tribal row, only too glad to be back to savagery again.

Like the Fijians, who were at one time the fiercest and most brutal cannibals of the Pacific, and who are now a peaceful and respecting nation, worthy of the crown that owns them, the Tannese will in all probability "train on" into a really fine race, as soon as they can be restrained from continuously murdering each other on the slightest provocation, and induced to clean their houses and themselves and live decently and quietly.

The yam gardens were weariful pictures. In one that we passed nearly all the women had blackened faces the Tannese sign of mourning. The yam garden was a waste of parched and powdery earth; the bush around was burned yellow and brown; the pale-blue sky above quivered with the fierce midday heat. Stolid and streaming with sweat, the women worked dully on, breaking off for a few minutes to stare and wonder at the visitor, and then continued their heavy task.

BUSHMEN COMING TO SEE A WHITE CHILD

FASHIONS IN ERROMANGA, NEW HEBRIDES

FURTHER READING

Tom Coffman's *Nation Within: The Story of America's Annexation of the Nation of Hawaii* (1998) reveals full information on the takeover by the U.S. government of the Kingdom of Hawaii. Robert Nilsen, J.D. Bisignani, *Big Island of Hawaii Handbook: Including Hawaii Volcanoes National Park, the Kona Coast, and Waipio Valley* (3rd ed.; 1998) covers the geography, natural history, culture, customs, and arts of the largest Hawaiian island.

Gavan Davis's *Shoal of Time: A History of the Hawaiian Islands* (1968) ranks as a thorough study of Hawaii during the 19th century. *Hawaii: a Literary Chronicle* (1967) edited by W. Storrs Lee is an excellent anthology of pre-annexation travel accounts. James Michener, in his nearly 1,000-page epic novel *Hawaii* (1959) presents a fictional account of the first migration to Hawaii. It is dramatic and informative. The incidents of the voyage are well within the bounds of accepted tradition.

See also Moana Tregaskis, *Hawaii* (1996); Hans Hoefer and Leonard Lueras, *Hawaii* (1989). Each volume contains chapters on 19th and early 20th century Hawaiian history and culture.

INDEX

108 INDEX

Clothing (*cont.*)
    of Yap, 80, 87, 91–92
    See also Ornaments/jewelry
Coconut oil, as safeguard against colds, 50
Coconuts/coconut trees
    disease, on Yap, 89
    grove, appearance of, 47
    iron as fertilizer for, 46
    Mark Twain on, 47
    as measure of wealth, 45
    in Nauruan legends, 43
    Stevenson on, 47
    stipule, 43
    toper, 34
    uses of, 43, 46, 50
    See also Copra
Colonial Sugar Refining Company, 98
Communication, 58
Copra
    and drought, 45
    drying, in sun, 55
    importance of, 29–30
    New Hebrides production of, 103
    original method of making, 29
    output of Marshall Islands, 95–96
    uses of, 106
Coral reef, 6, 7, 9
    British boring expedition, 46–47
    and natural formation of phosphates, 30–32
    pinnacles, on Nauru, 43
Creighton, Joseph, 67

Dakua, 100
Dance
    in New Britain, 12
    in New Hebrides, 104
    in Ponape, 57, 60
    ru-ong of Marshall Islands, 92
Darwin, Charles, 72
De Brum, Joachim, 94, 95
Disease
    dysentery, 97
    malaria, 13

native suseptability to, 50
small pox, 71
venereal, 92

Ear stretching, 71, 75
Easter Island, 16
Education
    in Mariana Islands, 88
    in Marshall Islands, 88
    mission schools, 92
    in Nauru, 37

Fiji
    climate, 97
    clothing, 101
    crime, 98
    forests, 13–14, 100
    geography, 97
    government, 98
    insects of, 97, 102
    music, 98
    nanga ceremony, 17
    natives, characteristics of, 98, 111
    population, 98
    rainfall on, 13
    vanilla cultivation, 100, 101, 102–103
    yanggona drink, 98, 100
Fishing
    with bow and spear, 33
    fish dance costume, 24
    with fish traps, 31
    live storage in lagoons, Nauru, 39
    net casting, 49
    with nets, fully clothed, 95
    shooting, New Hebrides, 109
Fison, Reverend Lorimer, 17
France, pre-war possessions of, 20
Frigate birds. *See* Noddies
Funafuti, 46–47

Germany
    Nauru under, 27, 28–29, 33–34

CONTRIBUTORS

General Editor FRED L. ISRAEL is an award-winning historian. He received the Scribe's Award from the American Bar Association for his work on the Chelsea House series *The Justices of the United States Supreme Court*. A specialist in American history, he was general editor for Chelsea's *1897 Sears Roebuck Catalog*. Dr. Israel has also worked in association with Arthur M. Schlesinger, jr. on many projects, including *The History of the U.S. Presidential Elections* and *The History of U.S. Political Parties*. He is senior consulting editor on the Chelsea House series *Looking into the Past: People, Places, and Customs*, which examines past traditions, customs, and cultures of various nations.

Senior Consulting Editor ARTHUR M. SCHLESINGER, JR. is the pre-eminent American historian of our time. He won the Pulitzer Prize for his book *The Age of Jackson* (1945), and again for *A Thousand Days* (1965). This chronicle of the Kennedy Administration also won a National Book Award. He has written many other books, including a multi-volume series, *The Age of Roosevelt*. Professor Schlesinger is the Albert Schweitzer Professor of the Humanities at the City University of New York, and has been involved in several other Chelsea House projects, including the *American Statesmen* series of biographies on the most prominent figures of early American history.